THE
DEPARTMENT CHAIR'S
ROLE IN DEVELOPING
NEW FACULTY INTO
TEACHERS AND SCHOLARS

ESTELA MARA BENSIMON
University of Southern California

KELLY WARD
Oklahoma State University

KARLA SANDERS
Buena Vista University

ANKER PUBLISHING COMPANY, INC.
Bolton, Massachusetts

THE DEPARTMENT CHAIR'S ROLE
IN DEVELOPING NEW FACULTY INTO
TEACHERS AND SCHOLARS

ISBN 1-882982-33-9

Composition by Lyn Rodger, Deerfoot Studios
Cover design by Lyn Rodger, Deerfoot Studios

Anker Publishing Company, Inc.
176 Ballville Road
P. O. Box 249
Bolton, MA 01740-0249

www.ankerpub.com

The Department Chair's Role in Developing New Faculty into Teachers and Scholars

About the Authors

Estela Mara Bensimon is the associate dean of faculty at the University of Southern California's Rossier School of Education and codirector of the USC Center for Urban Education, an interdisciplinary research center focusing on urban education issues in Los Angeles. She is also coprincipal investigator of the Project on Faculty Evaluation and Compensation and a professor in the division of Education Policy and Administration. Prior to joining USC, she was the principal investigator on a five-year study on organizational change for the National Center on Postsecondary Teaching, Learning, and Assessment. Her current research and teaching focus on faculty compensation, academic leadership, organizational change, and urban colleges and universities. Her publications have appeared in *Change, Review of Higher Education, Journal of Higher Education, Liberal Education,* and *Harvard Education Review.* She is the coauthor of *Redesigning Collegiate Leadership: Teams and Teamwork in Higher Education* (with Anna Neumann) and *Promotion and Tenure: Community and Socialization in Academe.*

Kelly Ward has been an assistant professor of higher education at Oklahoma State University since fall 1999. Prior to that, she was on the faculty at the University of Montana where she was also the director of the student volunteer center and the director of faculty development for the integration of service learning throughout the higher education system in Montana. Her areas of scholarly interest are junior faculty development, the service role of faculty, and the integration of service into the curriculum.

Karla Sanders is the director of the Center for Academic Excellence at Buena Vista University in Storm Lake, Iowa. She is responsible for the university-wide assessment efforts, meeting the needs of students with disabilities, managing the tutoring and study skills center, and coordinating the learning community program. Her PhD is in English from The Pennsylvania State University where she was the editor/conference coordinator for the National Center on Postsecondary Teaching, Learning, and Assessment.

This book is dedicated to Peggy Heim,
a generous advisor and mentor
to beginning scholars of higher education.

CONTENTS

FOREWORD

For most of the past decade, the faculty—as distinct from the universities and colleges that employ them—have been the focus of unprecedented criticism and complaint by a suspicious public grown leery of privilege and indulgence. While lack of understanding and misguided interest in improved student learning account for much of this unwelcome attention, the inquiries, complaints, and generalizations about faculty work have created an atmosphere of antagonism, rendering the professoriate the most vulnerable it has been since the 1950s. That's the bad news. The good news is that something is being done about it—including this book.

Within the next decade, some experts estimate that nearly half of the current faculty will retire or leave the academy. Who will replace them and why? Who will be attracted to the special rigors of academic life when esteem for the profession is low, when salaries are even lower by comparison with other highly educated professions, and when the patient investment of 15 to 20 years of life and income—from baccalaureate to tenure—seems immeasurably long? Moreover, who will manage this transition with the care, order, and vision necessary to sustain the intrinsically rewarding calling most of us attach to the work we do as faculty?

Many will be involved, but department chairs will inevitably occupy the pivotal position at the level where most faculty connect personally to their institutions and to the profession—at the level of the department and the discipline. Estela Bensimon, Kelly Ward, and Karla Sanders have written *The Department Chair's Role in Developing New Faculty into Teachers and Scholars* partly in anticipation of the growing importance of recruiting and retaining new faculty. They recognize the crucial role chairs will play in the process of repopulating, remaking, and repositioning the American academy.

They also understand that no matter how much we may take success for granted, we have not done an especially good job of developing our faculties in the past. The envy of the world, American higher education has excelled in no small measure because, for the most part, it has had the luxury of an exorbitant workforce for the better part of three decades. While there have been spot shortages and periods of diminished applicant pools, most colleges and universities have been able to select among sometimes embarrassingly large pools of qualified candidates and have, as a consequence, taken a somewhat cavalier attitude toward the development of their faculties.

Some universities have taken pride in the number of applicants they attract—and reject—in parallel with student applications for admissions. Others have cited statistics about the denial of tenure as a measure of quality. And most have taken for granted that better applicants are in the wings to replace casualties lost along the way from recruitment to retirement.

At my institution (a research university), for example, about half of the faculty hired in tenure-track, probationary positions are not considered for tenure six years later. Some are hired away, some leave academe altogether, some change faculty positions for clinical ranks or administration, and some are counseled into leaving without regard to alternatives; of those who remain, another 5% to 20% are given terminal appointments instead of tenure. In conversations with provosts of other research universities around the country, I have learned that these informal statistics are typical—when they are even known.

While the experience at colleges and comprehensive universities is somewhat different, the attrition rate is still surprisingly large. There are not many professions which endure, let alone prosper, when they demand as many years of preparation and as many years of probation before awarding full status to such a small number of their colleagues. Not only is the practice inefficient and costly, it is inconsistent with the values of community and collegiality we claim as special privileges of the academy.

Intense, daunting, and lengthy as it is, the process of recruiting, hiring, orienting, nurturing, and retaining new faculty is seldom examined, barely understood, and largely ignored. The authors have undertaken the challenge of considering this process explicitly. They have described a complete process, but they have wisely conceived of it in stages with meaning to the faculty member who is new: managing the recruitment and selection of new faculty; developing new faculty in the first year; and developing faculty beyond the first year. In turn, each of these three stages has discrete steps and components. This new book seeks not only to categorize and name the parts of the process, but it offers the tools needed to adapt habit and intuition into effective management practices. Properly understood, these steps—no matter how superficially familiar—can help department chairs achieve the mission and objective of their own units, as well as those of their colleges and campuses.

Essential as the total process and its component parts may be to institutional viability, the whole process belongs to no one, except possibly the department chair. Special person that she or he is, the department chair most likely was a member of the faculty only a year or two earlier or is in the last year of a term; few chairs who recruit and hire new faculty colleagues remain in office long enough to congratulate the successful candidates on receiving tenure and promotion. Moreover, professional development for chairs is less common than faculty development. Even essential institutional processes are left to the intuition of newly recruited chairs, and the most likely trainer for a new chair is the department secretary or administrative aide. Critical components of the process tend to fall through bureaucratic cracks or between the terms of chair appointments or the three stages described here. Such disconnects then create gaps in the individual lives of faculty who are trying to see their lives as continuous, whole careers, not discrete decisions which somehow accumulate into a dossier which wins tenure at the conclusion of a somewhat Delphic reading of the contents.

Colleges and universities depend on the energy and imagination of new colleagues to sustain and advance themselves in an increasingly competitive intellectual, knowledge-based, global service economy. To the department chair falls the responsibility and the opportunity to take ownership of the critical process that begins with recruitment and culminates with tenure—or a comparable rite of passage for different but equally important tracks that lead to continuous academic employment even without tenure. Experienced chairs will find that the three parts of this book offer fresh ideas and new ways of considering habits and routines; new chairs and prospective chairs will find a complex process laid out into component parts, each articulated with others so that an idea as abstract as "developing" new faculty can actually seem concrete and practical.

Estela Mara Bensimon and her colleagues have not prepared a manual or a guidebook (alas, and thankfully, there can be no useful *Department Administration for Dummies*). Instead, they have offered a framework for reflective self-critique and a distillation of best practices that most department chairs can adapt to design intentional policies and procedures for the effective—but locally focused—recruitment and retention of new faculty.

Similarly, deans or associate deans assigned responsibility for managing these activities will appreciate the insights and the practical possibilities for introducing or refining consistent practices across units. And those institutions fortunate enough to have a person charged with and supported in overall faculty development will be able to use the book for their own administrative workshops to help prepare new chairs or to renew and refresh incumbent chairs.

In their own work and experience, the authors represent and reflect the full range of wisdom needed to assemble a truly effective tool kit: the introspection of a new faculty member, the comprehensive overview of a professional developer concerned with teaching, and the practice of an administrator responsible for having prepared a productive faculty for a research environment. In addition, Estela Mara Bensimon's own extensive scholarly research on faculty roles adds depth to the analysis and description that grow out of experience. This is an important and timely work which will have a major impact on institutions wise enough to use it.

William M. Plater
Dean of the Faculties
Executive Vice Chancellor
Indiana University-Purdue University, Indianapolis

PREFACE

Everything seems to happen at the departmental level in this institution, and your chair can make your life miserable or wonderful. I am lucky because my chair has been very supportive of me. He always encourages me to show him my work. He is very complimentary. When my teaching evaluations come back and they're positive, he comes in and tells me; he gives me strokes for that kind of thing. He reads my work and gives me lots of comments.

This excerpt comes from an interview with a Mexican American female assistant professor in a large and prestigious research university in which she described her chair. All of the assistant professors interviewed in this particular department shared her positive opinion of the chair. Unfortunately, not all chairs are viewed as positively by assistant professors—not because they are not liked, but because of the things they fail to tell assistant professors or to do to make their adjustment less stressful and uncertain. In order to work effectively with junior faculty, chairs need to establish strategies for junior faculty development that include a clear view of what it takes to mentor new faculty from their first through their sixth year on the tenure track.

THE IMPORTANCE OF DEVELOPING NEW FACULTY

Of the many responsibilities that department chairs have, the one that has the greatest departmental and institutional consequences is hiring new tenure-track faculty and seeing them through tenure. Faculty are the institution and determine whether an institution develops a good reputation for teaching, for scientific advances, for service to the community, or for innovative practices. Faculty are the most valuable and expensive asset of colleges and universities. Consequently, in hiring and managing faculty development, department chairs have one of the most challenging institutional responsibilities. Yet, surprisingly, most department chairs are not well prepared to carry out this role effectively. Consistently, studies of tenure-track faculty have revealed that there is an unstated assumption that newcomers to the profession know how to accomplish what is expected of them. The reality, however, is that new faculty who have a clear idea of how to structure their roles in order to survive the probationary period appear to be the exception. More commonly, new faculty quickly become over-whelmed by the many demands placed on them for teaching, advising students, setting up their labs, establishing relationships, and figuring out the do's and don'ts. They often lack the time management skills needed to maintain a balanced schedule or the experience to know how to prioritize, and as they become more stressed, their ability to stay focused and organized lessens. Beginning faculty not only have to learn how to be teachers, scholars, and institutional citizens, but they also have to learn a whole new language, new procedures, and a new institutional culture.

Based on our research as well as from our different vantage points—one as a tenure-track assistant professor in a research university, one as a director of teaching development at a small teaching-oriented liberal arts college, and one as associate dean at a research university—we have become more aware of the lack of structures to facilitate the entry of new-comers. The absence of structures is in part due to the decentralized nature of institutions of higher education where the responsibility for orienting newcomers may be dispersed and left up to the discretion of each department. It is also the case that department chairs are typically not profession-al administrators, and unless their institutions have facilitated their partici-pation in special training programs for higher education administrators—such as Harvard's School of Education management institutes for higher education leaders, the Kansas State University academic chairpersons con-ference, or special seminars held at conferences sponsored by the American Council on Education, the American Association for Higher Education, the Council for Independent Colleges, and various discipline organiza-tions—they must learn on the job. Consistently, the information we and others have gathered in interviews with tenure-track faculty and academic administrators in all types of institutions leaves no doubt that in most places the socialization of new faculty, unlike, for example, student assess-ment, is not an institutionalized practice. On the other hand, there is also considerable evidence that institutional leaders are recognizing that the "sink or swim" approach to junior faculty is detrimental to the institution. Department chairs are the first to admit that they lack training and do not feel prepared for many of the roles they are expected to play. Department chairs who participated in a national study identified the need for training on how to "evaluate faculty performance," "encourage professional development activities of faculty," and "recruit and select faculty" as a high priority (Gmelch et al., 1992).

The expectation that department chairs be more intentional about the socialization of new faculty has created a need for practical information that is rarely provided in the higher education management literature. In this book we do just that: We walk department chairs through each of the critical socialization stages, beginning with hiring and ending with promotion and tenure. We draw extensively on published and unpublished interviews conducted by William G. Tierney and Estela Mara Bensimon for a project on new faculty funded by the Lilly Endowment and TIAA-CREF and reported in *Promotion and Tenure: Community and Socialization in Academe* (1996). With a few exceptions, the great majority of quoted excerpts come from actual interviews conducted as part of this research project in colleges and universities throughout the country.

We also rely heavily on the work of others, most particularly Robert Boice's *The New Faculty Member*, a "must read" book for all junior faculty.

The purpose of our book is to help chairs with the do's and don'ts in the three critical stages of junior faculty socialization: 1) recruitment and hiring; 2) the critical first year; and 3) evaluating the performance of new faculty. To accomplish this, we translate research into concrete advice and activities; we make extensive use of real-life situations; we integrate institutional materials that we have found to be helpful; and we provide generic examples of letters, checklists, and orientations that can be readily adapted to individual contexts. Additionally, we draw on our own experiences as two new assistant professors and a more senior professor who as associate dean is responsible for faculty hiring, promotion, and tenure.

THE ORGANIZATION OF THIS BOOK

The book has three parts:

Part I consists of three chapters in which we discuss all possible details of managing the recruitment and selection of new faculty, including the search process and organizing the on-campus interview, making the offer, and establishing a relationship before the new hire arrives on campus.

In Part II, we discuss how to manage the arrival of the newly appointed professor; specifically, we address the question of "What can department chairs do to facilitate the entry phase for new faculty?" The main topics in this part are formal orientation activities and the chair's role in developing new faculty to be effective teachers and productive scholars.

Part III discusses the role of the chair as mentor, both as it relates to facilitating collegiality in general and for women and faculty of color more specifically. This part also examines the chair's role in helping junior faculty develop as teachers and scholars beyond the first year, including a detailed description of the chair's role in guiding the newcomer through the mid-probationary review to the evaluation for promotion and tenure.

The academic labor market for the first time in many years is creating an influx of new faculty into the full-time nontenured, but tenure-track, ranks. This influx represents either an opportunity lost or gained: lost if new faculty are not socialized positively into their departments as to create a "win-win" situation for the new faculty member and the campuses they are joining; gained if faculty have positive experiences, earn tenure, and contribute to the profession, the department, and the institution. Not every new faculty member is likely to earn tenure, nor should all earn tenure. However, emphasis on the new faculty member's development and success creates a more positive situation for all concerned with the process. At any given time, departments, and consequently their administrators, are likely to find themselves in some aspect of the recruitment and evaluation process of their faculty. This process is inherently stressful, but it does not have to be one that is negative. The socialization of new faculty is an opportunity, perhaps like none other, for department chairs and their faculty to shape future directions of their department. *The Department Chair's Role in Developing New Faculty into Teachers and Scholars* is designed to make this unique opportunity easier and more organized for the department chair.

ACKNOWLEDGMENTS

This project was made possible by a generous grant from TIAA-CREF. The authors wish to thank Dr. Peggy Heim, former program officer at TIAA-CREF, for her long-time commitment and dedication to developing the professional careers of women in the academy. Peggy Heim opened many a door for us, for which we are most grateful.

REFERENCES

Boice, R. (1992). *The new faculty member: Supporting and fostering professional development.* San Francisco, CA: Jossey-Bass.

Gmelch, W. H., Burns, J. B., Carroll, J. B., Harris, S., & Wentz, D. (1992). *Center for the Study of the Department Chair: 1990 Survey.* Pullman, WA: Washington State University.

Tierney, W. G., & Bensimon, E. M. (1996). *Promotion and tenure: Community and socialization in academe.* Albany, NY: SUNY Press.

Estela Mara Bensimon
Kelly Ward
Karla Sanders

PART I

MANAGING THE RECRUITMENT AND SELECTION OF NEW FACULTY

When I went for the interview I met the chair, and the man who will be the next chair, and the man who is the dean and the man who's been in the department the longest time, and the man who teaches religion, and it was like a little club of men. I just met with the senior men in the department. I didn't meet any junior faculty. I didn't meet any women. I know there were women in the department, but they didn't schedule me to meet any of them. They didn't take me out to dinner the night before. They didn't give me breakfast. I actually wrote the schedule down myself while the chair read it to me. I assumed that there was an internal candidate and they were just going through the motions. But they ended up offering me the job.

> *[Same professor, a few weeks later] I came for the inter-*
> *view here, and it was the most thoughtful of all the five cam-*
> *pus interviews. They did things like giving me 20 minutes to*
> *myself between meetings with people. At the other place, I*
> *had 45-minute meetings with people starting at 8:30 a.m.*
> *and going through until seven at night without a break.*
> *Here people escorted me from one place to another, so that I*
> *got to meet people without feeling as if they were interview-*
> *ing me. In my schedule they had the names of the persons*
> *that would take me to each meeting and the name of the*
> *person who would pick me up.* (Tierney & Bensimon,
> 1996, p. 75)

The speaker in the excerpts above is a newly appointed assistant professor, who, as one might expect, accepted a position at the second institution, where she was treated more collegially. Much to our surprise, however, she accepted the second institution's offer even though she would have earned a substantially higher salary at the first institution (Tierney & Bensimon, 1996). In this section, we provide information that will help department chairs effectively manage the recruitment and hiring process. Our purpose is to assist chairs through this process so that prospective candidates will come away from the experience with the realization that "this is a good place to get started in my academic career."

The chair's role in the recruitment and selection of faculty is a critical one. According to Gmelch and Miskin (1995, p. 19), "Deliberate and careful selection of new colleagues has more to do with the growth and well-being of your department than any other action you may take." The selection of a new faculty member represents adding someone new to the culture of the department. However, the recruitment and selection of candidates is not an isolated act. We view the recruitment and selection phase as the first stage of a prospective colleague's initiation into the culture of the department and institution. The interview serves as the primary means by which the hiring department determines who among the candidates meets their expectations and who is likely to be a good colleague and department citizen. Candidates will also form impressions about the institution based on the interview. The organization of the interview, who participates, and the kinds of questions that are asked will influence the candidates' perceptions about the institution and whether they think they can fit in. A candidate will take an institution as seriously as the institution takes itself. A sloppy interview process reflects indifference, while a well-organized interview reflects respect for a potential colleague as well as concern for the well-being of the department.

The recruitment and selection of faculty, according to Gmelch and Miskin, consists of a three-stage cycle. The first stage involves setting up the search with a focus on planning; the second stage refers more to the design of the search, including the record-keeping aspects; and the third stage consists of the actual selection, including conducting the interview, making the offer, and completing the search. Although we will discuss aspects that span the three stages, we will primarily concentrate on stage three. Accordingly, Chapter 1 focuses on the elements of a well-organized search and interview, and Chapter 2 discusses negotiating the elements of the offer. In Chapter 3, we discuss the chair's role in assisting the newcomer to resolve personal relocation concerns that are associated with a move to a new location and position. Chapter 4 focuses on how the chair can help prepare the new faculty member for teaching, research, and service at the new institution.

REFERENCES

Gmelch, W. H., & Miskin, V. D. (1995). *Chairing an academic department.* Thousand Oaks, CA: Sage.

Tierney, W. G., & Bensimon, E. M. (1996). *Promotion and tenure: Community and socialization in academe.* Albany, NY: SUNY Press.

CHAPTER 1

ORGANIZING THE SEARCH FOR A NEW FACULTY MEMBER

The dean kept me waiting for 45 minutes, and when I finally did meet him, it [the interview] was just pleasantry. It was clear he didn't know who I was, that he was just going through the motions.

─────

It [the interview] was a blur. They kept me so busy I was not able to get nervous. I don't know what advice I'd give about changing it. It's just a gamut that you run through. [1]

Organizing a search that shows the department at its best is hard work and requires attention to details that are frequently overlooked. Surprisingly, despite the significance and expense of a search, there is very little information to assist chairs in its organization. Searches typically consist of forming a committee, writing a job announcement, placing it in professional publications, reviewing the applications, holding interviews with the candidates whose applications show the greatest promise, and offering the position to the most qualified candidate. Searches also consist of activities that are often overlooked: finding qualified candidates in non-traditional areas, involving the whole department in the process, finding ways to make on-campus visits successful, putting the department's best foot forward, and evaluating what the department really needs in a new faculty member.

We view the search for a new faculty member as an instrumental and symbolic act. The instrumental aspect points to the administrative details that will make the search organized and efficient. The symbolic aspect points to the messages—positive and negative—that are conveyed by the interactions that take place among the candidate and the hiring department and institution between the time the applicant inquires about the position and the conclusion of the search process.

According to Tierney and Rhoads (1994), "The recruitment and selection process serves as a rite of passage for faculty candidates as they seek organizational entry. The process is one of aligning values between organizational goals and objectives and candidates' skills, abilities, and interests" (p. 40). Annette Kolodny, the former dean of humanities at the University of Arizona, reminded the department chairs in her institution at the start of each new search "that the relationship that we have with this person begins at the interview process. Even if you are not going to hire this person, you may want to hire him or her in ten or five years. But if you do want to hire the individual, this is where the relationship starts, and it has to start positively" (personal interview with Bensimon, spring 1994). Taking Kolodny's advice begins with a well-managed search process that gives the prospective candidate a positive, albeit realistic, view of your campus community and your department. The following pages outline ways in which to foster this positive concept.

THE CHAIR'S ROLE IN MANAGING THE SEARCH PROCESS

Recruiting a new member of the faculty is much more than simply adding a new colleague to share teaching and service responsibilities. It is also an opportunity to bring about desired changes by recruiting colleagues with particular areas of expertise that the department needs. Vacancies also provide an opportunity to achieve greater diversity in the composition of the faculty. To take advantage of the search process as a strategic opportunity, chairs have to take into account the composition of the search committee, the content of the position announcement, and the organization of the interview so as to attract the kind of candidate the department needs. For example, if the department has no women on the faculty and the chair feels this is an opportunity to recruit a woman academic, he has to be cognizant of how to manage the interview process to demonstrate that the department can welcome women as academics and treat them as colleagues.

THE SEARCH COMMITTEE

The candidates' first impressions of the department will be influenced by their interactions with the faculty who make up the search committee. Thus, depending on what messages the department wishes to convey to prospective candidates, chairs need to consider who will serve on the committee. A committee that includes only full professors conveys one type of message; a committee that has senior and junior faculty, men and women, minorities, and students conveys a different kind of message. Creating search committees that are gender and race balanced is much more important today than in the past, yet in many institutions, the number of women and minorities who can be called on to serve on committees is still small. Kolodny dealt with this challenge without overtaxing women and minorities. She provided women and minority faculty with release time to compensate for their service on search committees, or she "borrowed" women and minority professors from other departments within her college. According to Kolodny, her strategy worked well "because the search committees were so differently composed, they read the applications differently," which made the pool of finalists much more diverse than in the past (personal interview with Bensimon, spring 1994).

Frequently, department chairs form committees with individuals who are alike in their attitudes, values, and disciplinary perspectives. Having a committee made up of people who get along well will make the search easier, but it also increases the chances of finding candidates who resemble the committee members. A department that is made up of individuals who have like experiences, intellectual orientations, and views of the academy runs the risk of becoming stagnant. A vacancy in the department provides an opportunity to be future-oriented, and for this reason it is important that department chairs have the courage and insight to put together a committee that accurately reflects the tensions that should exist (Murray, 1993). Such tensions may give candidates a sense of the invigorating nature of intellectual activity within the department, which can enhance the positive view desired.

THE POSITION ANNOUNCEMENT

Like the composition of the search committee, the position announcement also conveys important information about the department and the candidates it wants to attract. For example, one of Annette Kolodny's goals as

FIGURE 1.1

Sample Position Announcement

The Faculty of Humanities at The University of Arizona is composed of seven departments of languages and literatures, as well as several interdisciplinary programs, and offers degrees in 15 languages. *It has taken a leadership role in curriculum innovation and sustained affirmative action policies* (emphasis added).

All faculty enjoy the opportunity to participate in the activities of the Southwest Center, the Southwest Folklore Center, the Mexican-American Studies and Research Center, and the Southwest Institute for Research on Women. There are also opportunities for interdisciplinary affiliations with the American Indian Studies Program, the African-American Studies Programs, and the Women's Studies Program. Dean Annette Kolodny has encouraged cross-departmental and interdisciplinary efforts.

Tucson, Arizona is a community of diverse peoples and cultures. Applications from women and members of all underrepresented groups are especially welcome. We seek individuals with a demonstrated record of teaching and scholarly excellence.

dean at the University of Arizona was to increase the number of women and minorities on the faculty. Rather than simply saying that the university is an equal opportunity/affirmative action employer, one of the announcements in *The Chronicle of Higher Education* explicitly welcomes women and minorities to apply (see Figure 1.1).

Like Kolodny, Gmelch and Miskin (1995) also recommend that the job announcement be more intentional about reflecting the spirit of affirmative action. Rather than simply including the standard equal opportunity statement that is required by law on most campuses, they suggest including a statement that reads, "The department is particularly interested in appointing an individual who will enhance our efforts to address ethnic and cultural diversity issues, as well as our efforts to build collaborative relationships with the institution's constituencies" (p. 30). Whatever department goals your institution might have for the new hire, those goals should be reflected in the position announcement. In the case of the University of Arizona, Dean Kolodny expressed the institution's goal to increase its faculty's diversity.

The University of Arizona announcement has been carefully crafted to be inviting to ethnic minorities and women by highlighting the varied opportunities for involvement in interdisciplinary work; it also indicates that the dean in particular is committed to diversifying the faculty, and it informs potential applicants that the city is multicultural and multiracial. University of Arizona statistics for the years 1988 through 1992 suggest that the combination of efforts to diversify the faculty may have contributed to an increase from 41 to 77 women and an increase from ten to 30 ethnic minority professors in the Faculty of Humanities. Clearly, the efforts of Kolodny and the department chairs who worked with her paid off.

In addition to the language of the position advertisement, chairs also need to consider where to place job announcements. Attracting a comprehensive applicant pool requires not only placing an ad in *The Chronicle of Higher Education*, but also in disciplinary newsletters and journals, on appropriate professional listservs, at national and regional conferences, and in specialized journals. Areas of the country that may have difficulty attracting a large applicant pool should also consider placing the announcement in regional newspapers and sending it to colleagues in the area for nominations. The expense of such widespread publicity will pay off in the breadth of the applicant pool.

Affirmative Action

In addition to departmental desires to diversify its faculty pool for cultural and pedagogical reasons, there are also legal requirements associated with federal affirmative action policy that apply to most educational institutions. Federal requirements call upon search committees to make a "good faith effort" to develop an applicant pool that as much as possible reflects the available talent in the field that is inclusive of women and minorities. The department chair's role is to inform search committees about campus policies and perspectives on affirmative action in addition to federal regulation.

Once a committee is formed and charged with the hiring of a new faculty member, have the committee review affirmative action guidelines for the campus. These guidelines vary in terms of formality. On some campuses, once assigned, search committees are required to meet with an affirmative action officer to discuss strategies to make a "good faith effort" at diversifying the applicant pool, provide rationale for who is interviewed, and provide rationale for who is ultimately selected. Other campuses are less formal in their approach and simply rely on the good will of department chairs and their committees to come up with the best group of applicants possible in addition to selecting the best candidate.

Regardless of their requirements in terms of affirmative action in the search process, affirmative action offices are typically a good resource to help committees identify a strong and diverse applicant pool. For example, the Affirmative Action Office at Oklahoma State University has a recruiting resource guide that provides search committees with suggestions on where to find qualified and diverse applicants for faculty positions. These suggestions include ways to find and/or post information on appropriate Internet sites and lists, organizations that target minority job applicants, a list of historically black colleges and universities with graduate degree programs, and information about alumni who have agreed to assist in recruiting women, minorities, and, in some cases, individuals with a disability. While affirmative action policies vary considerably by campus, our intent here is to remind department chairs of the importance of learning these policies and assuring that search committees adhere to them in the search and selection process.

THE SCREENING PROCESS

Once the position announcement has been placed, the search process continues with two distinctive steps: 1) initial screening and 2) determining a long shortlist (10 to 12 candidates) to investigate in order to winnow down the pool into a list of three to four candidates to interview.

Initial Screening

For the initial screening, a letter of application and curriculum vitae may provide sufficient information to develop a long shortlist of candidates. Depending on the amount of information that the search committee wishes to review, the published job announcement will direct applicants to submit a letter of application and curriculum vitae, or it will require additional documentation of the applicant's accomplishments. Examples of the kinds of materials that can be requested include essays in which candidates are asked to write about their philosophy of education and teaching, samples of course syllabi, teaching evaluations, copies of articles, descriptions of research in progress, and samples of artistic creations. Some institutions also request that the candidates solicit letters of reference at the time they submit their application materials. Regardless of materials called for, it is important to keep information organized and easily accessible to committee members.

The following scenarios illustrate this part of the process and provide examples of responses that will facilitate the screening process to arrive at a long shortlist.

Scenario: The history department at a small liberal arts college advertises a faculty position and receives over 200 applications. This is the first time that the department's chair and administrative assistant conduct a faculty search, and they are unprepared for the sudden flood of applications.

Response: The department's administrative assistant can designate a special file cabinet or drawer for the search. As applications come in, each one is placed in an individual file. The applicant's file can include a checklist to keep track of the materials that have been submitted and the status of the application. A letter acknowledging receipt of the application and indicating the status of the application (i.e., missing materials) should be sent to the candidate within a week of receiving the application. Maintaining a master list—perhaps on a spreadsheet—with the names of the applicants and other relevant information such as race, gender, and degrees makes it easier to manage a large number of applications.

Scenario: The search committee is asked to review the applicants' folders and to recommend who among the candidates should advance to the next stage of the search process. When members of the search committee realize that there are 200 folders to be reviewed, they complain and ask the chair to come up with a simpler process to get the prescreening done quickly.

Response: The chair creates a checklist to help the members of the search committee review each of the applicants more systematically. The checklist helps the committee members complete the prescreening quickly and efficiently.

In a simple checklist the search committee can indicate whether 1) the letter of application addresses the needs stated in the job announcement, 2) the curriculum vita reflects the qualifications and experiences deemed appropriate for the job, and 3) the letters of reference are current and discuss the applicant's qualifications in relation to the stated requirements for the position (Gmelch & Miskin, 1995, p. 31). Members of the search committee can then be asked to indicate for each candidate whether to advance or eliminate them from this stage of the search. When there is a lack of consensus about a candidate, the committee can review the candidate's file again and determine the reasons to keep the individual in the search or determine the disqualifying characteristics.

For candidates who are disqualified, indicate the criteria they failed to meet. Doing this at the front end will save a lot of time when the search is completed and a report has to be submitted to the institution's office of personnel or affirmative action. A list of elimination codes that can be adapted is given at the end of this chapter.

The Long Shortlist of Candidates

Individuals who make it to the long shortlist, usually no more than ten, can be asked to submit supplemental materials if they have not already done so. The type of materials will vary on the basis of institutional type and requirements for the position. If the employing institution is a research university, the supplemental materials will likely include publications or a description of the applicant's research agenda. Institutions that are primarily concerned with undergraduate teaching may ask the candidate to submit a videotape of their teaching or teaching evaluations. Additionally, this is the time when it is advisable to check the candidates' references more thoroughly. Candidates can be advised that a member of the search committee will be making telephone calls to the individuals they have listed as references. Even if the candidate has submitted letters of reference, it is a good idea to follow up with a telephone call. Many individuals who provide letters of reference may provide a more candid and useful assessment in a conversation than in a letter, particularly if the individual is the candidate's dissertation advisor. At least two members of the search committee should be assigned to call the references of one candidate, so that the references are heard and interpreted from more than one person's perspective. At the end of this chapter is a standardized telephone reference form.

The results of the reference checks can help the search committee to agree on which candidates should be invited for an on-campus interview. Usually three or four candidates are invited for an interview, but the number can go as high as eight or as low as one, depending on the quality of the candidate pool, the institution's resources, and the amount of time that faculty are willing to invest in the search. Obviously, as the number of candidates invited for on-campus interviews grows, the more expensive and time-consuming the search becomes.

The department chair is usually the person who calls the candidates and lets them know they are on the shortlist and are being invited for an on-campus interview. After the initial call from the chair, the actual details to arrange for the visit can be handled by the department's administrative assistant or another member of the search committee.

The candidates who have been eliminated from the search should be notified in a timely manner. They should be thanked for their interest and informed that they were not selected for an interview.

PREPARING FOR THE CANDIDATE'S INTERVIEW

Despite its importance, interviewing candidates is often looked on as a burdensome task for which few are prepared in any kind of formal way. In our interviews with faculty and department chairs, we found that inexperience in organizing the on-campus interview can turn the search into a very unpleasant and disappointing experience. A faculty search is an expensive and time-consuming activity and requires serious planning for two types of activities: 1) the substance of the interview and 2) the logistical arrangements.

The Substance of the Interview

In preparing for the substantive aspect of the interview the chair can guide the search committee in the development of a common interview protocol so that each candidate gets asked the same questions about teaching, service, advising, and scholarship, as well as questions about his or her favorite leisure activities. Preinterview planning can include developing some of the following items:

- Questions department members will ask each candidate and who will ask specific questions

- Designation of who asks what questions

- Clear criteria that will be used by members of the search committee to rate the candidates

- Ground rules that clarify committee members' roles in the interviewing process

- Clear delineation of the decision-making process for recommending candidates for further consideration

The use of a uniform interview protocol at first may appear artificial, but having a protocol makes it more likely that the interviews will not be derailed by questions that are irrelevant or that will not help the committee determine the candidate's qualifications and interests. A clear protocol also helps avoid posturing by faculty members who want to impress the candidate, and it reduces the likelihood of asking rhetorical questions that cannot be answered. Similarly, closed-ended questions such as "Did you apply to this department because you like to teach?" are less useful than open-ended questions such as "What motivated you to apply for this position?" (Gmelch & Miskin, 1995, p. 41). Finally, it is illegal to ask personal questions related to age, marital status, health, religious preferences, or other matters not job related. These ground rules need to be reviewed with all those involved in the interview and campus visit process.

Evaluation of a candidate benefits from getting as much feedback as possible. In advance of the interview, ask parties involved to write an evaluation that will become part of the data the search committee uses in its decision-making. This may include evaluations of open presentations, student sessions, and open meetings with the faculty. Collecting comprehensive evaluations is also a way to involve as many people in the search process as possible.

Sample Questions to Use to Rate Candidates

- Does the candidate appear different on paper than in person? If so, what personal characteristics contributed to a negative impression?

- How did the candidate's energy level appear? Active? Average? Lethargic?

- Did the candidate give the impression that he or she was nervous, relaxed, unsure, confused, defensive, or rigid?

- What was seen in the candidate's facial expressions? Openness? Arrogance? Puzzlement? Pleasantness? Boredom? Alertness?

- Were the expected weaknesses of the candidate confirmed by the interview? Were new ones discovered?

- Were the strengths confirmed? Were new strengths revealed? Did the candidate show genuine promise?

- Did the interview reveal any unexpected problems? (Tucker, 1992, p. 175)

The Logistics of Setting Up the Interview

Once the committee and others who will interview the candidates understand the questions and procedures that have been put into place, the chair or the administrative aide for the search should contact the candidates concerning their campus visits. In order to help candidates prepare for their visits, the department can prepare a packet of information including such items as the institution's bulletin, strategic plan, course descriptions or catalog, and any other information that conveys the department's goals and values. In addition, the packet should include a map of the institution and some basic information about the town or city (these materials are usually available from the Chamber of Commerce or, in the case of large cities, in travel guides or in city-specific magazines such as *Los Angeles Magazine* or *New York Magazine*). It is also useful to provide the candidates with the web site addresses for the institution and the department.

Candidates will have different needs for information and different personal circumstances. Given individual differences, it is important to guard against making assumptions based on stereotypes. For example, rather than trying to guess whether applicants will want information about schools for children, it is safer to provide a packet of information that would meet the needs of the candidate whether or not he or she is a parent of school-age children, single, straight, gay, or lesbian. The purpose of the information should be to let candidates know about the community as well as to provide them with a sense of the institutional and local climate and whether they are likely to be comfortable. For example, gay and lesbian faculty (regardless of whether they are out or not) are likely to be concerned about the institution's policies with regard to benefits for domestic partners and nondiscriminatory practices vis-a-vis sexual orientation, while faculty with children are likely to be concerned about day care and family insurance.

The travel arrangements are usually made by the institution and, if possible, the airline ticket as well as the hotel should be prepaid. Keep in mind that candidates for assistant professor positions are likely to be recent PhDs with limited funds. The person who makes the travel arrangements should determine the individual's preferences (e.g., smoking/nonsmoking room, dietary restrictions, seating preference on the plane) in order to make the candidate's visit comfortable. Some institutions may decide to house the candidate in on-campus housing; this is fine if the housing has the amenities one would expect in a hotel; otherwise uncomfortable lodging can add to the stress of the interview.

At least a week prior to the interview, candidates should receive a typed itinerary for their visit. The first item in the itinerary should be the time of arrival at the airport or train station and the name of the person who will meet the candidate and drive them to the hotel. The chair of the search committee should meet the candidate. If it is impossible to meet the candidate in person, do not tell him or her to grab a taxi (for someone coming from a small town to, say, La Guardia Airport in New York City, summoning a cab could be overwhelming). Instead contract a car service; the fare is usually about the same or just slightly more than a taxi, but the driver will usually meet the person at the gate and assist with luggage. The itinerary should provide the home telephone number of the chair of the search committee in case of an emergency.

If the formal interview begins in the morning, it is likely that the candidate will arrive in the afternoon or evening prior to the interview. This is a good time to have an informal meeting with the candidate and provide him or her with more background information about what to expect in the following two days and to explain who is whom in the interview schedule and what their roles are in the search. The schedule should include the following information:

- The name and title of each individual with whom the candidate will meet individually as well as in meetings organized around breakfasts, luncheons, and dinners. Individual interviews can be scheduled for 45 minutes with a 10- to 15-minute break to provide time to walk from one office to another or use the rest rooms. Students can be designated as escorts to guide the candidate through the appointments.

- A room should be available with coffee, soft drinks, and water where the candidate can relax during breaks.

- In addition to the department chair, the candidate should have individual meetings with the dean, with faculty from within the department or from other parts of the institution who share similar research or teaching interests, and with a group of students.

Too often the involvement of deans in the interview process is perfunctory, and the questions that they ask demonstrate lack of knowledge about the candidate. Chairs can assist deans by providing a summary of each candidate's background, highlighting significant information. A dean who participates actively in the interview process, such as being present at the candidate's presentation and participating in the discussion or being present at one of the luncheons or dinners, sends a very different message than the dean who does not seem to know what questions to ask the candidate, is excessively late for the appointment with the candidate, takes phone calls during the interview, or appears distracted or disinterested. The dean's behavior can help create or destroy the air of collegiality that should be fostered during the interview process.

- At least one lunch or dinner should be only with junior faculty. An all-women or minority lunch or dinner is also an option in the case of women or minority candidates in order to give them a sense of the community and get a frank assessment about the institutional climate and what they can expect if they are offered and accept the position. This is also a good strategy if the candidate is a woman or a person of color and the department is predominantly male or has no minorities.

Sensitivity to the particular needs of candidates can make a big difference in how the institution is judged by the candidate. For example, an African American male told us, "One of the good things that happened was that I was introduced to other black faculty who were not part of the interview process, and that was very helpful. It was helpful because they talked about what it means to be a faculty person [at this institution] from a black perspective, and you know, they tell you things off the record, so you get the message. They'll give you the real deal, and on balance, they were very positive about this place" (Tierney & Bensimon, 1996, p. 106).

- The itinerary should also provide time for a guided tour of the campus as well as a tour of the city or neighborhood, preferably with an experienced real estate agent.

Key Factors for a Successful Interview

I had two days of interviews. I started out at nine in the morning, and I taught a class, and then I had separate interviews with probably eight to ten people. There was a luncheon with a faculty group and I also had a meeting with the dean, and I ate dinner with the head of the department. I was impressed. It was a real comprehensive kind of interview. For instance, I had to teach a class, and that was interesting to me. The faculty were knowledgeable about me and interested in my employment. (Tierney & Bensimon, 1996, p. 106).

This excerpt comes from an interview with a minority female assistant professor at a selective liberal arts college, and we include it here to illustrate the elements of an effective interview. From this excerpt as well as the one presented at the opening of this chapter, we can extrapolate at least six elements that are needed for a successful interview.

- Individual meetings with faculty, administrators, and students; and informal meetings around meals. It usually lasts two days.

- A printed interview schedule is provided prior to the candidate's arrival with names of people who are doing the interviewing and the person who will take the candidate from meeting to meeting and from campus to the hotel.

- Meals are organized as opportunities for more relaxed exchanges to get to know the candidate.

- As part of the interview, the candidate meets with the dean.

- The interview provides various opportunities to assess the candidate (e.g., giving a demonstration class or making a professional presentation as well as one-on-one interviews and meals).

- The effort put into planning the interview, from making the travel arrangements to the scheduling of interviews, lets the candidate know that he or she is important and that your department and institution are humane places to work.

There is nothing particularly unique about these elements, and the initial reaction may be to dismiss them as just common sense and good manners. However, as we mentioned earlier, most individuals in academic administrative positions have limited experience in managing searches and, in too many cases, institutions do not provide handbooks or guidelines on how to conduct an interview or on best practices for faculty search committees.

Throughout this chapter we have emphasized the importance of being aware of the messages that are conveyed in how the search is managed.

The Job Talk

The job talk is customary in most interviews, and it usually consists of a session in which the candidate gives a formal presentation on his or her research. In some institutions, the job talk may also include a pedagogical colloquium which requires candidates to give a formal address on the pedagogy of their discipline or an informal discussion about teaching and curriculum, which is a means of assessing a candidate's knowledge of teaching. For example, the history department at Stanford University encourages candidates to put together syllabi for courses they would like to teach. As part of this discussion, members of the search committee can ask questions about undergraduate teaching, advising, how the courses they would like to teach fit into the existing curriculum, and how the candidate would teach a particular book or theme.

We believe that it is important for candidates to discuss their research as well as their teaching. Teaching and research presentations or demonstrations allow departments to evaluate different capabilities of candidates. In order to make the job talk as stress-free as possible, let the candidate know the type of presentation that is expected and inquire about special audiovisual aids. If the candidate plans to use PowerPoint or similar presentation software, it can be very unsettling to find out at the last minute that the department's secretary forgot to make the arrangements, leaving the candidate to improvise. It can also be unsettling for the candidate if only a very few people show up for the presentation. It is the responsibility of the department chair to communicate to the members of the department the importance of selecting a new colleague and being actively involved in the process. The presentation should be treated as a formal occasion, and walking in or out during the presentation should be discouraged. It is also important to intervene if faculty members take advantage of a candidate's presentation to posture or to dominate the discussion or to show off their knowledge of the subject. While it is expected that the candidate will field questions, there is a difference between honest intellectual exchange and intellectual jousting.

Concluding the Interview

The candidate should have an exit meeting with the department chair in order to go over questions that may have emerged over the course of the interviews. The chair should also inform the candidate about the timetable for the search and when he or she should expect to hear about the outcome. Many chairs also take this time to discuss salary and benefits with the candidate. A member of the search committee should drive the candidate to the airport. This will provide additional time for wrapping-up and addressing any final questions of the candidate.

After negotiating the minefields inherent in the search and interview process, the chair's attention must next turn to completing that process by hiring one of the candidates. In the next chapter we will address the issues that arise in making the job offer. (Also see Perlman and McCann, 1996.)

CHECKLIST: CANDIDATE'S DISQUALIFICATION

☐ Failed to provide minimum components of application

☐ Failed to respond to requests for additional information

Degree consideration
☐ Did not possess required degree as advertised

☐ Degree not in compatible field with needs of department

Teaching requirements
☐ Area of specialization overlaps with current faculty

☐ Candidate's teaching not suitable

Research/scholarship requirements
☐ Insufficient publication (exhibition/performance) record

☐ Lack of demonstrated research/performance skills

☐ Not published adequately given length of time in profession

(Source: Gmelch & Miskin, 1995, p. 35)

SAMPLE PROTOCOL FOR TELEPHONE REFERENCES

Nominee/Candidate _____

Reference Contacted _____ Name _____

_____ Title _____

_____ Address _____

_____ Phone _____

Contacted by _____ Date _____

Introduction

This call is in the way of a confidential request for information on (name of candidate), who is being considered by (name of university) for the position of assistant professor, in the (Department of English in the College of Liberal Arts). We would appreciate any information you may be willing to provide to us, and we shall consider such information to be of a confidential nature.

1. How do you evaluate the candidate's potential:

   (a) to build a record of distinction in his/her area of specialty?

   (b) to be an effective teacher and advisor for undergraduate students?

   (c) to achieve tenure?

   (d) to work with graduate students?

2. How do you rate the candidate's attributes in the areas of

   (a) commitment to innovation?

   (b) enthusiasm?

   (c) interpersonal relations? (with faculty, students, etc.)

   (d) follow-through?

   (e) scholarly production?

3. If there was a vacancy in your department, would the candidate be considered as a serious candidate?

4. As a tenure-track assistant professor, what are the most likely obstacles the candidate is likely to encounter?

5. Would you please identify for us others who may know the candidate and who might be contacted?

   [GET NAMES, ADDRESSES, AND TELEPHONE NUMBERS IF POSSIBLE.]

CHECKLIST: WHAT TO AVOID DURING THE INTERVIEW

☐ Being late for the candidate's interview. This is particularly grave if the person who is late is a dean or department chair because it sends the message of a cavalier attitude to the candidate who may expect similar treatment as an employee.

☐ Making inappropriate jokes or sexist or racist remarks.

☐ Not showing up for a scheduled meal with the candidate.

☐ Telling the candidate that you have a tennis date or other type of frivolous engagement which will prevent attending the candidate's job talk.

☐ Not including students in the interview schedule.

☐ Including a senior professor who is openly hostile and antagonistic to the candidate's specialization in a lunch or dinner meeting.

☐ A low turnout of senior faculty to the candidate's job talk or class demonstration.

☐ Indulging in excessive drinking.

☐ Being excessively combative or disagreeable in the discussion following the candidate's job talk or class demonstration.

☐ Asking inappropriate or overly personal questions.

REFERENCES

Gmelch, W. H., & Miskin, V. D. (1995). *Chairing an academic department.* Thousand Oaks, CA: Sage.

Gmelch, W. H., & Miskin, V. D. (1993). *Leadership skills for department chairs.* Bolton, MA: Anker.

Hutchings, P. (1996). The pedagogical colloquium: Focusing on teaching in the hiring process. *AAHE Bulletin, 49* (3), 3-4.

Kolodny, A. (Spring, 1994). Personal Interview.

Murray, J. P. (1993). Hiring: Back to the basics. *The Department Chair, 3* (4), 16-17.

Perlman, B., & McCann, L. I. (1996). *Recruiting good college faculty: Practical advice for a successful search*. Bolton, MA: Anker.

Roberts, R. (1996). A report from the Stanford history department. *AAHE Bulletin, 49* (3), 3-6.

Tierney, W. G., & Bensimon, E. M. (1996). *Promotion and tenure: Community and socialization in academe*. Albany, NY: SUNY Press.

Tierney, W. G., & Rhoads, R. A. (1994). *Faculty socialization as a cultural process: A mirror of institutional commitment*. ASHE-ERIC Higher Education Report No. 93-6. Washington, DC: The George Washington University School of Education and Human Development.

Tucker, A. (1992). *Chairing the academic department: Leadership among peers* (2nd ed.). New York, NY: ACE/Oryx.

----

[1] We draw extensively on published and unpublished interviews conducted by William G. Tierney and Estela Mara Bensimon for a project on new faculty funded by the Lilly Endowment and TIAA-CREF and reported in *Promotion and Tenure: Community and Socialization in Academe* (1996). With a few exceptions, the great majority of quoted excerpts come from actual interviews conducted as part of this research project in colleges and universities throughout the country.

CHAPTER 2

NEGOTIATING THE JOB OFFER

Notably, the negotiation process was handled very well by the chair, as far as salary and the job conditions. My advisors helped me a bit, but I was not very good at the process. Jonathan, the chair in our department, kind of nudged me along. I found him to be sort of fatherly, and he told me some of the things that I might ask for. I had an hour-long private meeting with him and he said, "Here is what a package might look like." He had named some things that I would have never considered. He told me that a computer package would very likely be part of an offer. He suggested a travel budget, and I didn't know that I could ask for this in addition to travel for conferences. This summer I will be able to go to England to do my research in a special collection. I also got summer stipends for three years and they paid all of our moving expenses.

THE JOB OFFER

At the conclusion of the interview process, the search committee recommends to the department chair and, usually the dean, the ranked candidates that best meet the qualifications for the vacant position. Just as the interview communicates important messages about the department culture, the actual job offer—what it consists of, how it is communicated and negotiated—will also influence the candidate's relationship to the department and institution.

Questions to Address at the Time the Job Offer Is Made

Gmelch and Miskin (1995, pp. 42-43) observe that if the chair has been listening to the candidate throughout the process, he or she will be able to address the following questions when making the formal offer of the job.

- Is the candidate's spouse or partner in need of employment? If so, are there employment opportunities available in the community?

- What type of schooling is needed for the candidate's children?

- What does the candidate need to achieve tenure?

- What type of housing does the candidate desire? What are the candidate's interests in teaching, research, and service?

- What shortcomings might the candidate perceive to be inherent in your institution?

- What is the candidate's need for collegiality? For autonomy?

- What type of start-up costs will be incurred by the candidate's needs in terms of computers, labs, and research assistance?

- What needs might exist in terms of consulting or overload pay?

The job offer stage consists of 1) negotiating a comprehensive compensation and support package and 2) facilitating relocation. We use the term "negotiating" intentionally to highlight that in many institutions compensation packages are negotiated on an individual basis, and not all recently minted doctorates have been taught the rules of this game. In an institution where individual negotiations are conducted, it is the chair's responsibility to see that candidates are not unfairly disadvantaged because they have not been socialized in the negotiation of contracts. The department chair's actions during the posthire process can make the biggest difference in establishing a healthy working environment for the department's new hires.

Because of socialization and background discrepancies—gender, race, culture, upbringing, past working environments, or graduate training—not all new faculty will know what to ask for, when or how to bargain, or that bargaining is accepted or even expected. The custom of individual salary negotiations has been shown to place women at a disadvantage, particularly those who have not been mentored as graduate students and instructed on negotiation rituals and courtship customs that are common in hiring practices in the academy. Women often receive starting salaries that are lower than those of their male peers because they do not know what to ask for or how to negotiate. One assistant professor told us, "I didn't think about negotiating. I felt lucky that I was getting a tenure-track job. I wanted to say to the chair, 'I am really happy to come, and I want the job, and you have really been nice,' and bring it to a closure" (Tierney & Bensimon, 1996, p. 79).

If salaries are negotiated on an individual basis, it is particularly important to guard against creating inequities. For example, in a university that has no salary schedule, we found one assistant professor earning a salary of $55,000 while all the other assistant professors were earning salaries in the mid $40,000 range. A disparity as large as this one is only justifiable if the individual is particularly qualified and has demonstrated that he or she will immediately make very valuable and significant contributions. Because of the inherent problems with an individualized system of salary negotiation, some deans and chairs have instituted guidelines to make the system more fair or to eliminate it entirely. In one institution, the dean promulgated a policy that assured all new faculty members substantially the same salaries, research budgets, and travel allowances.

Department chairs need to be explicit about the conditions of employment. Clarity of expectations smoothes the new faculty member's transition to campus and prevents later allegations of unfairness. As the senior administrator of the department, the chair needs to document all employment arrangements and is ultimately responsible for assuring that the outcome of the negotiations is adhered to and that the department is accurately represented. When the individual being appointed has held tenure-track positions at other institutions, the letter of appointment should specify whether the previous experience counts toward the number of required probationary years for tenure. The chair should explain to the candidate the advantages and disadvantages of asking for credit for previous experience on the tenure track (e.g., a shortened probationary period gives the candidate less time to build up the dossier).

In addition to the base salary, the letter of offer should specify the equipment (e.g., computer, lab equipment) that will be purchased for the candidate or the amount of money that will be at the disposal of the candidate for such purchases. It should also specify whether the individual will be assigned a teaching or research assistant, how many hours per week, and for how long (i.e., the first year only or throughout the probationary period); the amount of travel allowance and the conditions, if any, for its use; release time during the probationary period; and opportunities for extra income such as summer school teaching. The letter should also indicate reimbursement for moving expenses and, if available, housing allowances. In areas where housing is very expensive, such as in New York City or Los Angeles, institutions frequently provide funds or low interest loans to enable the purchase of a home. Department chairs should have all of this information available. If they are not sure what is available, the institution's treasurer or chief fiscal officer should be consulted.

The department chair should anticipate that the newcomer will have questions about relocation and should provide much of this information at the time the appointment is made. Frequently asked questions by newcomers include: Does the institution provide a monetary stipend for the move? What is that stipend amount? What does it cover? How are moving expenses reimbursed or paid? What receipts, contracts, and so forth are required by the accounting office? Does the institution have a contract with a specific carrier? Inevitably, not all questions can be anticipated, so between the time of the appointment and the actual relocation, the new professor should have a contact person—either within the department or in another institutional office—who can accurately and specifically answer questions related to relocation. (Also see Perlman and McCann, 1996.)

Questions to Answer in a Letter of Appointment

In order to make all arrangements clear to both the new faculty member and the department, the chair should draft an itemized appointment letter confirming the allocation of facilities and resources promised in pre-employment negotiations. A list of items to include in a letter, as well as a sample letter, follow.

- What should happen between the time the job offer is made and the arrival of the new professor?

- What kinds of needs will the newcomer have, and how can the department chair be proactive?

- What can the new professor expect to encounter after arriving on campus?

- What is included in the offer? Provide a comprehensive list.

Note that this letter uses first names only in the signature; it is a good idea to establish department standards of address from the beginning.

Sample Letter of Appointment and Introduction

Dear Dr. Smith:

We are pleased to have you as a new member of the faculty. In order to make your transition to the department as smooth as possible, I want to reiterate the arrangements we discussed during our phone conversation.

Your office will be outfitted with a new PC and a laser printer. You will also have access to one-quarter time secretarial help from John Jones. Please feel free to contact John (phone number) with any procedural questions you might have.

Most faculty in the department teach five or six courses a year. We have arranged for you to teach only four courses in your first year. In the fall semester you will teach two courses: Intro Class, a class of about 70 students, with the help of an assigned graduate assistant, and a Teaching Methods course to advanced undergraduates (typically a class of about 25 students). Enclosed are the most recent syllabi for these courses, along with the names, phone numbers, and email addresses of faculty who taught the courses last year. If you have questions about organizing the courses, or need suggestions for texts, please feel free to contact me. When you get settled in, let's meet for lunch to see how things are going. I'll contact you sometime in the first couple weeks of the semester.

The transition to our institution is a substantial move for you, and I would like to make it as easy as possible. Based on your research interests, I have arranged with Evelyn Smith to act as a mentor/contact person for you. Her research interests are similar to yours, and she is pleased to answer any questions you may have about the department, the college, and/or the community. She will call you within the next couple of weeks to introduce herself and to assist you during the relocation period.

Also enclosed is some information I thought you may find useful to facilitate your transition to College town (a local paper, a Chamber of Commerce packet, list of local schools, and information about our faculty development program). I have also included a departmental faculty list, which describes scholarly and teaching interests and service assignments.

If you have any questions about the department, the college, or the community, please feel free to contact Dr. Brown or myself. I look forward to working with you this fall.

Sincerely,

Eric LaMarque
Department Chair & Professor

REFERENCES

Gmelch, W. H., & Miskin, V. D. (1995). *Chairing an academic department.* Thousand Oaks, CA: Sage.

Perlman, B., & McCann, L. I. (1996). *Recruiting good college faculty: Practical advice for a successful search.* Bolton, MA: Anker.

Tierney, W. G., & Bensimon, E. M. (1996). *Promotion and tenure: Community and socialization in academe.* Albany, NY: SUNY Press.

⊷⊷⊷ CHAPTER 3 ⊶⊶

PROVIDING INFORMATION BEFORE ARRIVAL: WHAT'S USEFUL FOR RELOCATION

The department chair arranged for me to come back and look for housing, and he had a group of faculty over for dinner to his house. It was nice, so different from the interview.

Usually a new assistant professor's appointment involves a relocation from one city to another, often to unfamiliar parts of the country or from small college towns to large metropolitan areas. The relocation also involves the anxieties of making a life transition and getting started in a career in an institution that may be very different from the one he or she is leaving. Once the offer has been made and accepted and the initial excitement settles down, the individual will wonder: Where will I live? Can I afford it? Will my spouse move with me? What are the job prospects for my spouse?

Too often it is at this critical point that the new professor fails to hear from the hiring institution. This is unfortunate because it is precisely at this time that the new professor is likely to have questions about the new position in addition to logistical questions about relocation to the new community. In this chapter we address the practical issues related to assisting the new faculty member's relocation, and in the next chapter we address providing information on teaching, research, and service before the new professor's arrival.

FINDING A PLACE TO LIVE

Some institutions will underwrite a post-hire visit for the candidate and his or her spouse or partner to help them search for housing and begin the relocation process. We know of one institution, for instance, where the department paid for a stay of several days for the candidate and his partner and provided them with a rental car and contacts to help the candidate's partner search for a job. In that same institution, a newly hired assistant professor was invited to spend a week with his family at a neighborhood bed and breakfast in order to find housing. During these visits, faculty in the department organized social events including dinners, a visit to an amusement park for the children, and a baseball game. Such consideration assures that the new hire begins to feel part of the department and creates a feeling of collegiality from the beginning.

The following scenario illustrates a typical relocation problem encountered by a new faculty member.

Scenario: Anne spends the summer preparing to move from Massachusetts to Texas. She must find daycare for her two-year-old daughter and enroll her six-year-old in first grade. Her husband quits his job and begins to search for a position in their new town. Because of the children, they have decided they need to buy a house. Since they are currently two thousand miles away, they must do this search long distance. Anne must take the realtor's word for the neighborhood and school district where the house they can afford is located. Their savings are meager, and they are not sure they have enough to make the minimum required down payment.

Response: This situation can be easily avoided by anticipating the kind of information new faculty will need based on their personal circumstances. Information on housing, schools, and daycare centers can be provided at the time of the interview or after the offer has been made.

Obviously, the most desirable practice would be to invite the new assistant professor and family back for a longer visit in order to search for a home and begin the process of settling into a new place. For departments with tight budgets, we recommend putting together a package of useful information. Large cities have a variety of publications that can be excellent sources for newcomers, and it is not hard to put together a very attractive and informative package, complete with web site information if available. Articles published in the local newspaper with titles such as "Making Sense of Los Angeles Neighborhoods," "The Best Public Schools in Iowa," or "Where to Bank" can be particularly helpful to the newcomer. Large bookstores usually have a section with books that are relevant to the local city, many of which are ideal for newcomers. It is also helpful to provide URL addresses to the local newspaper, chamber of commerce, and real estate agencies. At the University of Southern California's Rossier School of Education, new faculty members are provided with a copy of the *Thomas Maps to Los Angeles* (no one can survive Los Angeles without one), a book on restaurants, and the *Newcomer's Guide to Los Angeles* to help navigate the city.

In smaller cities where such resources may not be as readily available, the department could give a committee, a secretary, or a student the job of developing a handbook for newcomers. Three professors at Hamline University compiled a *Guide to the Perplexing: An Introductory Survival Manual for New CLA Faculty at Hamline* (Bell, Brock, & Gildensoph, 1993), which provides information in alphabetical order beginning with banks and ending with voter registration. The guide also includes essential information such as a description of all the university's directories and schedules, how to order textbooks, how to use voice mail, and so forth. These details may sound mundane and common sensical; nevertheless, they are frequently overlooked because they have not been standardized into an easy-to-use format. Another useful strategy is to assign a faculty member as the point person to assist the newcomer with relocation.

FAMILY ISSUES

I have concerns about time off for childbearing—stopping the clock. There is a strong pressure not to do this in my department, but I feel that the institution needs to be more aggressive in guaranteeing women this opportunity if it wants us to stay here.

A detail that must be taken into consideration is that the newcomer may have a spouse or partner who is also a professional and more than likely will need assistance in relocating. Note that heterosexuality should not be assumed, and it is important that the chair make clear the department and institutional climate for gay men and lesbians. This can be accomplished by being explicit about the institutional policy vis-a-vis sexual orientation, domestic partner benefits, as well as by including information on gay and lesbian groups and organizations on and off campus. The chair, through language and actions, has to create a climate that makes it safe for the individual to be "out" if he or she chooses to. The chair can help by informing the candidate of services provided by the institution to assist spouses and partners, by circulating their résumé, and by putting them in contact with individuals who can advise the spouse or partner on how to conduct a job search.

In today's professional climate, it is not uncommon for professional couples to have jobs in different cities and have a commuting relationship. Needless to say, commuting adds another stress to the relocation process, and department chairs can play a role in helping the candidate plan ways of making this work. We expect that some chairs may view the personal relationships and arrangements of candidates as something private or as "their problem." While this may have been true when commuting was an exception, it is now much more common, and department chairs can make it easier or harder—easier by openly discussing how commuting might work (e.g., clustered course schedules) and harder by not mentioning the issue at all.

For beginning female professors, the tenure and biological clocks are often concurrent, and it is important to provide information on institutional policies regarding family leave. The excerpt that begins this section illustrates the impact a new position may have on new professors' decisions to start a family. Most colleges and universities have provisions for stopping the tenure clock in the case of a major life-changing event (e.g., having a child, severe illness), so explaining those provisions can put the candidate at ease, particularly if she feels anxious about asking such questions. Likewise, many community college faculty are on a year-to-year contract and may be concerned about how parental leave would affect such a contract.

The following checklist provides a quick reminder of the kinds of information on family and relocation issues that may be of help to a new hire.

CHECKLIST: FAMILY/RELOCATION INFORMATION

☐ Explain the availability of funds for relocation and how to be reimbursed for relocation expenses.

☐ Establish a department contact person to supply information on relocation.

☐ Provide a packet of information on Realtors, schools, neighborhoods, utility companies, daycare facilities available on campus or in the area, places of worship, community organizations, and athletic facilities.

☐ Offer web site addresses (URLs) for Realtors and the local newspaper.

☐ Provide the newcomer with a subscription to the Sunday edition of the local paper for the three months preceding his or her move.

☐ Explain what the institution and department can provide in terms of assistance for spouse or domestic partner employment.

☐ Be specific about institutional benefits including provisions for domestic partners.

☐ Make clear under what conditions the tenure clock can be stopped.

☐ Provide information on special interest or religious organizations on and off campus.

☐ Include information on campus and community accessibility for faculty or their family members with a disability.

REFERENCES

Bell, C., Brock, R., & Gildensoph, L. (1993). *Guide to the perplexing: An introductory survival manual for new College of Liberal Arts faculty at Hamline*. St. Paul, MN: Hamline University.

Tierney, W. G., & Bensimon, E. M. (1996). *Promotion and tenure: Community and socialization in academe*. Albany, NY: SUNY Press.

CHAPTER 4

PROVIDING INFORMATION BEFORE ARRIVAL: TEACHING, RESEARCH, AND SERVICE

I had questions about my teaching, about where to order books, things like that, but I didn't want to seem like a "typical woman" who asks lots of dumb questions, so I never called anybody.

After I was hired I never received any information about what classes I was to teach. I knew I would be expected to teach six classes a year, but my department chair was not clear about what classes or how many students I would have. Needless to say, this made me feel a little apprehensive about teaching.

We talked constantly, from the time the chair hired me. He sent me syllabi, and I could ask him questions about what kind of courses to prepare. The chair was accessible, and I felt comfortable talking to him.

During the recruitment and selection process, the candidates who make the shortlist are in frequent communication with the chair of the search committee and others in the department while the arrangements for the interview are discussed and completed. However, it is not unusual that once the offer is negotiated and the contract signed, communication ebbs. Once the appointment has been made, it is largely the responsibility of the chair to manage the period between the time of the appointment and the official start of the position.

Recruits for new positions are usually notified in the late spring about their selection, with the expectation that they will assume the position in the fall semester. For a new professor who is faced with having to design new courses, teach and advise a diversity of students, contribute to institutional initiatives ranging from internationalizing the curriculum to using technology, and serve on faculty committees, the time they have in between the appointment and the actual start date is an excellent time for chairs to help new hires prepare for their new position and its responsibilities.

As the opening recollections from the three assistant professors demonstrate, some chairs make use of this time to help the newcomer in the transition whereas others may forget about the new professor until he arrives on campus. In this chapter we discuss the role of the chair in structuring this in-between period purposefully as the initial stage in organizational socialization. In another section of the book we dedicate more time to the ongoing socialization of new faculty in the areas of teaching, research, and service. Our point here is to focus on the time immediately before the position begins as a means to help acclimate and prepare faculty for their new position.

In the same manner that the recruitment and selection stage should be viewed in the context of a long-term relationship with the individual, what happens during the period following the offer but before the newcomer actually moves into his or her office also sets a tone for the relationship between the individual and his or her department. Obviously, newcomers will form impressions about their colleagues and the culture of the workplace based on whether the transition to their new position was planned or neglected. Being attentive to the transition stage for the newcomer is consistent with the collegial values we espouse and will help strengthen the department's esprit de corps.

TEACHING

New hires are likely to be eager to make a good impression on the department chair and will seek to appear confident and qualified, but even the most confident and qualified new professor will need basic information about the courses they will teach. The excerpts at the beginning of this chapter indicate that one of the new hires was not only left in the dark concerning teaching questions that needed to be answered, but was also made to feel like a troublesome nuisance. This can be avoided by a proactive response by department chairs.

Scholars of teaching and learning report that the components of effective teaching include 1) preparation and organization, 2) the ability to stimulate student thought and interest, 3) clarity, 4) enthusiasm, and 5) knowledge and love of content (Weimer, 1996). While department chairs may not be able to instill enthusiasm and love of content in new professors, they can provide new faculty with simple, learnable, low-risk techniques that can be put to use in the first months of teaching. "If the first experiences go reasonably well, faculty members will be motivated to continue to learn and develop as effective teachers" (McKeachie, 1994, p. 80).

Helping the New Professor Get Organized

As with any new position, a certain amount of anxiety is likely to be present no matter how experienced the new faculty member is in teaching. And the average new faculty member fresh out of graduate school has limited background in teaching. While some graduate students serve as teaching assistants or even teach their own sections of courses, there is typically very limited orientation and training in how to teach. The following scenario illustrates typical teaching pitfalls caused by anxiety and a new hire's ignorance concerning what questions to ask the department chair.

Scenario: Based on his graduate school experience, Bob assumes that his first-year teaching assignment will be courses similar to the ones he has taught in the past. When he arrives at his new institution three weeks before the fall semester begins, he learns that the courses he will teach include not only the introductory course he expected, but an advanced course in his discipline and a senior seminar (topic to be announced) as well. Instead of spending the summer preparing for these courses, Bob, because of his wrong assumptions, spent the summer playing golf.

Response: Send sample syllabi, book lists, and the name and phone number (and email, if used) of faculty who taught the course(s) previously. Ask the faculty member who has experience with that particular course to call the new professor. Offer information on course goals and how the course fits into the departmental and institutional requirements for students within the major and for those taking general education requirements.

To assist newcomers with teaching preparation and organization, provide them with Wilbert J. McKeachie's "Countdown for Course Preparation" from his seminal work, *Teaching Tips: Strategies, Research, and Theory for College and University Teachers* (McKeachie, 1994).

In helping the new professor prepare for the first teaching assignment, it will be important to describe the courses to be taught in the context of the entire department, including information on 1) the role of this course in the department, 2) whether other instructors are depending upon this course to provide specific kinds of background knowledge or skill (i.e., is the course a prerequisite), 3) who the students are, and 4) what students' current concerns are (e.g., self-discovery, social action, career preparation)

FIGURE 4.1

Countdown for Course Preparation

Three Months before the First Class

- Write objectives (chair can provide newcomer with samples of what are considered to be well-written course objectives)
- Draft a syllabus for the course
- Order textbooks or other resources students may need

Two Months before the First Class

- Work out tentative set of assignments for the students
- Decide what should be in the course outline or syllabus
- Choose appropriate teaching methods
- Check resources needing advance work
- Begin preparing lectures and other teaching activities

Two Weeks before the First Class

- Check on textbooks and library resources
- Check on enrollment projections
- Visit the classroom
- Prepare for the first class

Source: McKeachie (1994, pp. 9-19).

(McKeachie, 1994). Additionally, it is helpful to provide a profile of the typical student population in the general education courses taught in the department as well as the students enrolled in the major. Insider information on typical student preparedness, gaps in students' knowledge, average SAT or ACT scores, and so forth can help a professor who is new to the institution prepare her or his courses. New faculty will also find copies of the student course catalog and other brochures describing undergraduate and graduate requirements useful guides to learn about the department and institution as well as the student population in the department and at the university.

Stimulating student thought and interest. It is important for new professors to realize that what happens in the first 15 minutes on the first day of class can influence the rest of the semester. To help new professors orchestrate the first meeting and begin to create a strong learning culture in the classroom, we recommend providing them with a copy of McKeachie's Chapter 3, "Meeting a Class for the First Time" or Nilson's Chapter 7, "Your First Day of Class" (Nilson, 1998). This chapter provides advice on how to break the ice, introduce oneself to the students, explain the course syllabus and requirements, and generally how to get students involved from the first day of class.

Being clear. It is important for students to have a clear understanding of the rules of the classroom as well as of the criteria for evaluating their performance. The chair can help the new professor establish the procedures and policies for the classroom by sharing information on what is customary in the department. The syllabus should be clear on what the professor's expectations are regarding attendance, deadlines, lateness, and classroom decorum.

Another area where clarity is important is in the explanation of the course. Rather than provide students with a perfunctory and antiseptic description of the course (Weimer, 1996), chairs can provide new professors with course descriptions that effectively relate the course content to the students' interests. Faculty also need to determine critical course objectives—another area that can be problematic for the novice faculty member. If writing objectives is overly mechanical and uninspiring, Weimer (1996) suggests alternative ways of getting this done. One option is to imagine meeting students five years after they took the designated course and determining what one would like the students to remember. The second option is to determine the course objectives by writing up the final exam and considering what kinds of knowledge and skills the student would need to perform well.

The time between the job offer and the first day in the classroom is an ideal time for department chairs to impart information about teaching to new faculty. Taking advantage of this transition time is likely to avoid problems in the future. Chairs can use the Checklist: Providing Teaching Information at the end of this chapter to make sure they adequately prepare new faculty before they start teaching. This information can also be accompanied by any departmental or institutional information about teaching and any books or resource material on teaching.

In Part III we spend more time discussing the ongoing socialization and professional development of the teaching role of new professors.

RESEARCH

The day of my campus interview was so full and rushed, we never got to discuss my area of research in detail. So I was surprised and somewhat disturbed when I got here to learn that no one in the department really knows much about my research interest. In my field collaborating is critical, and at this point, I'm worried about how to get established. They gave me the impression that there would be no problem, but now I'm not so sure.

One of the greatest challenges for the junior professor anticipating a new position is deciphering institutional priorities and relative importance of teaching, research, and service. Although the emphasis placed on these responsibilities varies by institutional type, most faculty are required to attend to some type of balance among these areas. Of these three requirements, research tends to be the most ambiguous and produce the most anxiety. The exceptional faculty member is prepared to start a new position and "hit the ground running" on research, but most new faculty are unclear about expectations for research, how to get started, and building a coherent research plan (Boice, 1992). Department chairs can help with the transition to the new position by clearly articulating expectations for research at the institution and in the department, and by simply talking to the new faculty member about research and developing a research agenda.

By turning unwritten assumptions about promotion and tenure requirements that guide expectations for teaching, research, and service into stated policy, the department chair can demystify this part of the profession. While many new faculty will not hesitate to ask colleagues about teaching ideas or techniques, many people feel that inquiries about research indicate lack of skills. A common belief is that they—the junior faculty members—by virtue of their position should just simply know what to do when it comes to research. After all, they have the degree. However, research agendas and tenure requirements differ greatly among institutions, fields, and departments.

While new faculty know they typically have to initiate research right away in their new positions, they are far less certain about how to initiate the research agenda and whom to ask about tenure requirements for research. Also, in the midst of moving to a new location, preparing new classes to teach, and learning one's way around a new campus and a new city, research—because it lacks pressing due dates or anxious students clamoring for help—may be pushed aside. Boice (1992, 1996), in his research on new faculty, found that research, writing, and publication are often the first to be left by the wayside when a person is dealing with competing responsibilities. Both classes and committee meetings require a physical presence. Research is different in that it is largely a solitary effort, especially when a person is new to the profession and campus.

Scenario: Kathryn's current research area differs from her dissertation. She is eager to bounce ideas off colleagues and garner advice about where to start and how to design her study. When she reaches her new institution, she discovers after several casual conversations that no one she has spoken to is interested in this topic. Discouraged, she stops discussing her research with her colleagues, unaware that one of them has just published a book on a related topic.

Response: Provide a list which describes the teaching, research, and service agendas/interests of all department faculty so that new faculty can easily make those connections.

What can department chairs do between the time of hire and the actual relocation to the campus to help facilitate the transition of the new scholar? As described in the response above, providing new faculty with pertinent information about departmental colleagues' research is a good first step to initiating the research agenda. Such information should include pertinent scholarly activities, courses each has designed and regularly teaches, journals edited by department members, and ongoing professional activities like conferences attended or given. Such information lets the new hire know about scholarly work being conducted in the department and helps familiarize inexperienced faculty with the teaching and research networks of the discipline. Such information can also help avoid the disappointment expressed by the assistant professor in the excerpt that begins this section.

Department chairs can also help faculty meet institutional and departmental research expectations by learning more about the research interests of the new faculty member and arranging links with experienced faculty sharing similar interests. This linkage provides new faculty with a campus reference person to contact upon arrival on campus. A research mentor who contacts the new faculty member before arrival can help to pave the way for a new hire to manage research from the start. This will help avoid a pitfall most new faculty face—spending too much time on teaching, wanting to get involved in service as a way to acclimate, and overlooking research responsibilities. This may not seem like a problem at the outset, and it may not be. But it has the potential to become a cumulative problem (Corcoran & Clark, 1986). Faculty members who postpone initiating research while they get their courses set up and get to know colleagues on campus through committee work risk losing ground in the area of research. It can be difficult to make up this deficit as promotion and tenure draws near.

Imparting information prior to arrival about facilities and funding available to aid the new faculty member's research agenda is also important. Because attendance at annual meetings of the discipline is important to professional development, new faculty need to be made aware of how much travel funding they can anticipate from their department each year. Resources such as laboratories, computer facilities (including email and Internet access), libraries, and interlibrary loan should be spelled out from the beginning. Human resources in the form of secretarial support and teaching or research assistants should also be explained before a new faculty member arrives with unrealistic expectations based on previous experiences.

Department chairs can use the guidelines provided in the Checklist: Helping to Establish a Research Agenda at the end of this chapter to prepare faculty to meet the research obligations of their new positions.

SERVICE

Tenure and promotion in most colleges and universities is based on performance in teaching, research, and service. On many campuses, criteria for determining how well an individual has performed in the area of service are ambiguous and highly subjective. Moreover, the weight given to service in determining whether an individual merits tenure varies according to institutional types. In research universities, service is probably the area that counts the least whereas in smaller institutions service may be of considerable importance.

In addition to providing the new hire with information about research and teaching expectations at your institution, it is also helpful to explain the kind of service that faculty are typically involved in during the first year. Service may include serving on governing committees at the departmental or institutional level or additional consultation work in the community. While most people expect research and teaching obligations, service time commitments are often overlooked when planning for a new position. One of the biggest surprises many first-time faculty encounter is the number of required meetings and committee obligations that come along with the faculty position. As a department chair, you can help protect new faculty from being overburdened by service in their first few years. You can also inform new hires of the number and kind of service tasks expected of them as junior faculty members. Such information about typical departmental meetings, committees, and subcommittees within the department, college, or institution can give new faculty a fuller picture of the new position they will encounter.

Although institutional policies are not likely to mention good citizenship as one of the criteria for granting tenure, the fact is that department committees have denied promotion and tenure to individuals who do not demonstrate this quality. Good citizenship is highly subjective and is often used against scholars who do not conform to the expectations of senior faculty or who question the way that things are done. Chairs can help circumvent this ambiguity by clearly articulating service expectations for the first year. Further, it is important to articulate different types of service. Outreach-oriented service typically involves activities like applied research and evaluation and participation in disciplinary and professional associations. Institutional service is more focused on the campus level and includes participation in committees and other governance bodies.

In the last section of this chapter we discuss the role of department chairs in explaining service expectations to new faculty. First, we provide a comprehensive list of service activities drawn from several institutional documents. A list such as this will be helpful to new faculty who may not know much about service activities.

Outreach-Oriented Service: Sample Activities

- Conducting applied, directed, or contracted research
- Conducting program, policy, and personnel evaluation research for other institutions and agencies
- Consulting and providing technical assistance to public and private organizations
- Conducting public policy analysis for local, state, national, or international government agencies
- Informing general audiences through seminars, conferences, and lectures
- Appearing on television and at media events
- Acting as an expert witness and testifying before legislatures and congressional committees
- Editing newsletters
- Designing new programs
- Collaborating with schools, industry, and civic agencies
- Administering festivals and summer programs in the arts
- Planning conferences
- Holding a leadership position in disciplinary and professional associations and societies
- Serving on accreditation bodies, national examination boards, or governing boards and task forces

Citizenship and Institutional Service: Sample Activities

- Administrative responsibilities or program oversight
- Serving as chair or member of department, school, or campus committees
- Representing the institution on boards or in activities

- Participating in campus governance

- Student advising

Junior faculty who approach service too enthusiastically or too indifferently risk suffering negative consequences. The role of the chair is to help new faculty understand that doing too much service will get in the way of excelling in teaching and research, and even though service duties may be highly valued and appreciated, junior faculty are not likely to earn tenure on the basis of good citizenship alone. On the other hand, being nonchalant about service will send the wrong message to senior faculty who evaluate the assistant professor's performance. Even if a committee is not too important or is not known for getting much accomplished, the assistant professor who decides to miss meetings in order to do more important work runs the risk of being viewed as a noncontributing member of the department.

In some instances department chairs and senior faculty will warn a new colleague to limit time dedicated to service activities, but the admonishment is useless if the same people do not limit the number of committees the assistant professor is asked to serve on. Junior faculty are relatively powerless, and saying "No, I am not able to accept the invitation to serve on the task force" often is not possible. It is up to the chair to limit the number of committees a faculty member serves on. The onus needs to be on the department chair, not the new faculty member, when it comes to saying "no" to too many service obligations.

Participating in service activities can be of value to new faculty. It enables them to meet other faculty, to learn about the campus in a less formal way, and to get a sense of the community. Research by Robert Boice (1992) shows that productive faculty make it a point to network with other members of the campus community, as serving on a committee with an influential member of the faculty provides an opportunity to establish important and useful relationships. The department chair's goal in working with new hires is to help them achieve a balance among teaching, research, and service commitments.

Finding this balance can be particularly tricky for women coming into a department that is predominantly male or for professors from ethnic minority groups coming into departments that are predominantly white. Many committees call for diverse representation, and faculty who are the lone representative of their race or gender can quickly become overwhelmed with service responsibilities. Again, it is up to the department chair to help the new hire find a comfortable balance, enabling them to meet people in the department and on campus and become involved in institutional affairs without getting overburdened.

We conclude Part I of the handbook with some general checklists department chairs can use as they prepare for the new hire to join the existing faculty.

CHECKLIST: WHAT THE NEW FACULTY MEMBER WILL NEED TO KNOW BEFORE ARRIVING ON CAMPUS

- ☐ **Information about the position/campus:** Salary and benefits, including reimbursement for moving expenses; schedule of salary increases; scope of the position within the department and the department's position within the institution; department structure and other faculty members; when to arrive on campus; parking for faculty; institutional traditions/expectations. Provide any handbooks the department and/or campus has available for faculty (e.g., faculty handbook, student advising handbook).

- ☐ **Information about the area:** Housing/real estate information, including a real estate contact; information about schools and daycare sources; cultural and entertainment events/schedules; sporting events; transportation to area; local laws/ordinances that could affect one's lifestyle.

- ☐ **Information about the work environment:** Equipment provided in the laboratory or office, including computer availability, software, and support; office assignment and the name of officemate (if applicable); clerical support availability for research and teaching needs; email availability; office address and phone number.

- ☐ **Information about courses to be taught:** Course load, expected number of office hours per week, profiles of typical course sizes and students in those courses, sample syllabi and book lists, list of others who have taught the course recently, summer teaching requirements/availability.

- ☐ **Information about service expectations for the department and institution:** Committee work and the number a new faculty member may be asked to join, student advisor expectations, availability of a mentoring program, service exemptions for the first year on campus, schedule of department meetings generally held, yearly calendar.

☐ **Information about research aid:** Availability and frequency of research assistants; sabbatical leave structure; travel funding for junior faculty; availability of research tools and equipment, including library resources; availability of funds to support research at the department, school, or university/college level.

☐ **Information about personnel issues:** Payroll schedule, benefits, availability of insurance (including when it is effective), schedule of pay raises, and spousal and dependent benefits.

CHECKLIST: PROVIDING TEACHING INFORMATION

☐ Inform faculty of courses to be taught.

☐ Provide sample syllabi and/or book lists.

☐ Explain student population in general education courses and in the major.

☐ Inform new faculty on course requirements and other departmental offerings.

☐ Provide contact to other resources such as faculty who have previously taught the course.

CHECKLIST: HELPING TO ESTABLISH A RESEARCH AGENDA

☐ Provide information about research interests of faculty in the department.

☐ Match a new faculty member with an existing faculty member with similar research interests.

☐ Inform faculty about the availability of travel funds to support research endeavors (e.g., data collection) and/or to attend conferences.

☐ Explain the resources available for research in your field both on and off campus.

☐ Provide application materials for any research support available to faculty in the first year.

CHECKLIST: ORIENTING NEW FACULTY TO SERVICE ACTIVITIES

☐ **Explain what counts as service.** Provide new faculty with a list of service activities. Explain the difference between outreach-oriented service and service to the institution. Outreach-oriented service is more important in public institutions, particularly land-grants, and it can include applied research and evaluation, dissemination of knowledge, and formal involvement in disciplinary and professional associations. Service to the institution includes participation in committees, governance bodies, and other administrative duties.

☐ **Make service assignments.** Appoint new faculty to service activities within the institution that will not require additional work other than attending meetings. Assign new faculty to committees with faculty who can be helpful in their socialization. Let the new faculty member know who is who on the committee and their roles within the institution.

☐ **Protect women and minorities.** Women and minorities often get asked to do an excessive amount of service because of the need for representation on committees. It can be difficult for a new faculty member to say "no" when asked to serve on committees so be sure to "protect" women and minorities from being overburdened with service obligations.

CHECKLIST: NEW HIRE PREPARATION

Candidate's Name: _____

Office Assignment: _____

Officemate (if sharing): _____

Office Phone Number: _____

Email Address: _____

_____ Office cleaned and stocked with supplies

_____ Computer set up and working

_____ Software installed

_____ Laboratory completed and supplies ordered

_____ Email account established

_____ Office stocked with departmental/institutional phone
directory, informational sources (faculty handbook, where
to go for necessary information like ordering AV equipment for the classroom, sending interoffice mail, making
class handouts, etc.), and office supplies including departmental stationery

_____ Business cards ready to be ordered

_____ New grade book available

_____ Mailbox/slot ready

_____ Building and office keys made

REFERENCES

Boice, R. (1992). *The new faculty member: Supporting and fostering professional development.* San Francisco, CA: Jossey-Bass.

Boice, R. (1996). *First-order principles for college teachers: Ten basic ways
to improve the teaching process.* Bolton, MA: Anker.

Corcoran, M., & Clark, S. M. (1986). Perspectives on the professional
socialization of women faculty: A case of accumulative disadvantage.
Journal of Higher Education, 57, 20-43.

Gaff, J. G., & Lambert, L. M. (1996). Socializing future faculty to the
values of undergraduate education. *Change, 28* (4), 38-45.

McKeachie, W. J. (1994). *Teaching tips: Strategies, research, theory for college and university teachers* (9th ed.). Lexington, MA: D. C. Heath.

Nilson, L. B. (1998). *Teaching at its best: A research-based resource for college instructors.* Bolton, MA: Anker.

Tierney, W. G., & Bensimon, E. M. (1996). *Promotion and tenure:
Community and socialization in academe.* Albany, NY: SUNY Press.

Weimer, M. (1996). *Improving your classroom teaching.* Thousand Oaks,
CA: Sage.

PART II

DEVELOPING NEW FACULTY IN THE FIRST YEAR

I really felt welcomed when I first got to town for my new job. The department chair had a barbecue at her house with other faculty in the department and college. I got to meet everyone and their families at once which was a little overwhelming, but nice. The next day she [the chair] asked me to come to her office and we sat down and went over what I could expect with the onset of the new semester. I was glad we had this meeting because I had a lot of questions about getting started. She also showed me to my new office and introduced me to just about everyone in the building. She literally walked me through all the standard procedures in the office and the building. I felt welcomed from the start. When the semester got started I really felt informed and ready. I instantly knew I made the right decision to come here.

I had to get my own keys, computer, telephone, stationery. I didn't know there was a mailroom, and I only just got the key for it, more than a month after classes started. (Tierney & Bensimon, 1996, p. 80)

In preparing for the new faculty member's arrival, the chair referred to in the first excerpt succeeded in making the new professor feel valued. In contrast, the chair mentioned in the second excerpt made the new professor feel completely ignored and added to the stress of being in a new job and a new city. The extent to which a department is prepared for the arrival of newly appointed professors can make a great difference in their attitudes toward their colleagues and their department. Baldwin (1990) has suggested that "if the early years as a professor are unsatisfying, they can diminish enthusiasm and create a negative attitude that may persist throughout the career" (32). Clearly, if new professors feel neglected or unnoticed, they may opt to concentrate on furthering their academic careers and make a minimal contribution to the collective interests of the department or institution. As institutions face a more hostile environment and feel pressured to be more innovative and entrepreneurial, there will be a greater need for faculty to be more involved in making their departments adaptive to changing circumstances. Department chairs play a critical role in creating conditions that will induce or inhibit faculty belief, commitment, and loyalty to the department.

In view of the importance of creating collaborative departments, one would assume that chairs would make efforts to welcome their new colleagues. Surprisingly, however, new faculty experiences repeatedly suggest the contrary. In some cases the newcomer arrived to find that the chair was out of town, and no one had been informed that a new professor would be arriving. In other instances new faculty had to manage without an office and the equipment they were promised for months.

As mentioned in Part I, not all new faculty members, particularly women and minorities, have experienced graduate education as a process of socialization into the profession. For many, graduate education spends little or no time on the profession itself, focusing instead on the field of study. While many chairs may expect new faculty members to hit the ground running, they can do so only if their graduate careers socialized them to be savvy junior faculty. Unfortunately, many graduate programs do not address their students' next professional step after completion of their degree. Graduate training is simply inadequate preparation for understanding academic culture and the demands of a faculty position. In graduate school, students interact daily with departmental peers and professors; the tenure track, however, is a time of uncertainty and isolation. Leaving the familiarity of graduate school and the security of long-time relationships with professors and students, coupled with the pressures of getting established professionally, can be very unsettling. Many new professors are not well prepared for this transition and end up feeling overwhelmed during the first year. Expecting all new faculty to know what to do and how to respond to the many demands of their new position can unfairly disadvantage those who lack the academic capital needed to succeed. Accordingly, a major aspect of the chair's role is to facilitate the socialization of new faculty and help them develop the behaviors and habits that are associated with being a successful academic. Baldwin (1990) has noted that competence is the main concern for new faculty, and chairs can help their new colleagues learn to prioritize in order to become competent professors and scholars.

This part addresses the question, What can department chairs do to facilitate the entry phase for new faculty? Fink (1984) has shown that after their first year, two-thirds of faculty indicated that they wished they could have had a better orientation at the beginning of the year to provide information to questions they had, as well as answers to some questions they did not even know they should ask. In this part, we identify critical questions to answer in the early weeks of a new hire's arrival on campus. These questions have been organized into four categories which delineate the focus of each chapter in this section: professional/institutional questions, professional/departmental questions, teaching questions, and service and campus community questions. Chapter 5 outlines those questions a new faculty member may have about the institutional organization and culture, including some concerns about expectations for tenure and promotion. Questions about tenure and promotion have been addressed both at the institutional and departmental levels because so many institutions have interdepartmental committees, deans, and vice presidents who make these decisions in addition to the feedback provided by the department. We recognize, however, that such questions tend to be answered at the departmental or field level.

In addition to promotion and tenure questions that may arise at the departmental level, Chapter 6 also covers the areas of concern that arise within the department itself, including the day-to-day issues of who does what in the department and how things are handled administratively. Chapter 7 addresses questions that new faculty will need to have answered as they prepare to teach new courses or, for many disciplines, prepare to teach college-level courses for the very first time. Chapter 8 delineates concerns surrounding service and the campus community and how chairs can help new faculty use their time wisely. Each chapter addresses the issue of formal and informal orientations and includes a checklist of critical questions to be answered. The part concludes with a broader checklist of do's and don'ts for orientation activities.

Just as it takes a village to raise a child, so it takes a department to orient a new faculty member. Throughout this handbook we have addressed both formal (e.g., orientation) and informal (e.g., mentoring and collegiality) mechanisms to enhance junior faculty success. The final chapter in this part, Chapter 9, provides ideas and examples for ways to extend orientation and to involve all departmental faculty in activities that will help new hires throughout their entire first year. In particular, we focus on how mentoring can extend into the first year, providing faculty members with support as they encounter questions and difficulties.

Many of the questions outlined in this part—particularly those related to promotion and tenure—will be continual concerns for junior faculty. Because of the ubiquitous nature of many of these questions, we advocate mentoring beyond the first year, which will be discussed in Part III. However, we also recognize that answering as many questions as possible in the early days can help alleviate stress and can simply provide information the new professor requires in order to begin a new semester at a new institution.

References

Baldwin, R. G. (1990). Faculty career stages and implications for professional development. In J. H. Schuster & D. W. Wheeler (Eds.), *Enhancing faculty careers: Strategies for development and renewal* (pp. 20-40). San Francisco, CA: Jossey-Bass.

Fink, L. D. (Ed.). (1984). *The first year of college teaching.* New Directions for Teaching and Learning, No. 17. San Francisco, CA: Jossey-Bass.

Tierney, W. G., & Bensimon, E. M. (1996). *Promotion and tenure: Community and socialization in academe.* Albany, NY: SUNY Press.

CHAPTER 5

ADDRESSING PROFESSIONAL/INSTITUTIONAL QUESTIONS

When I got to campus I had a lot of questions. You know, things like: Whom do I ask for help with teaching ideas? Do people collaborate on research projects? Even really basic things like, What can I ask the secretary to do?

If I have a single complaint about this place, it's that I have no idea what the true expectations are, and they haven't been communicated to me. This is a major disappointment. I know there is always a trade-off between research and teaching, but I haven't had anyone be able to make clear to me what constitutes effectiveness in each area. I've asked other junior faculty members, but unfortunately they don't know either.

All new faculty on campus are required to go to an orientation that is organized by the provost. Basically, it is a half day of guest speaker after guest speaker talking about their offices and what they do. The presenters ranged from human resources to dean of students. Was is it helpful? Sure, it's helpful to know who's who and all that and to know who the other new faculty are on campus. I wouldn't say a half day is enough nor would I say that it helped me get a sense of the nitty-gritty of my job, and that's what I really needed my first days on campus. I pretty much had to learn as I went along.

Establishing a positive relationship with a new faculty member begins before he or she arrives on campus by providing information and resources necessary for relocation and the preparation of new duties (see Part I). This early information flow underscores the importance of communication for the new faculty member. Many chairs may offer an open door policy for newcomers to ask questions as they occur; other chairs will elect to provide new faculty with a department mentor who can answer questions as they arise; still others will rely on well-structured orientation programs to provide the necessary information. Whatever system works best for your department, it is essential that the new professor's questions be answered and that avenues for future queries be enunciated. In order to provide the most positive, stress-free first few months, those avenues should be readily available and welcoming to the new faculty member.

While seasoned professors may change institutions and know where to go to acquire various pieces of information, a new faculty member may not be aware of all the resources available on campus such as what offices handle what situations, or who within the department may be the proverbial font of information or informal keeper of departmental and institutional history and lore. By introducing the new faculty member to such resources, the chair can ascertain the successful flow of communication among department newcomers and more seasoned faculty.

In addition to providing information on the various campus services and offices, a complete orientation can help the new faculty member understand how information is transmitted and communicated throughout the department and the institution as a whole. Seemingly obvious information may not be so obvious to someone used to a different system at a previous institution or to someone new to the profession. These communication issues include questions such as: How do committees report on their meetings? How is the information that comes from the dean's office transmitted to the faculty? The provost? The president? What avenues of communication are encouraged? How will the new faculty member be evaluated? By whom? When? When should one's opinions be expressed?

CRITICAL PROFESSIONAL/INSTITUTIONAL QUESTIONS TO BE ANSWERED

The questions that follow in this chapter and the other chapters in this section illustrate typical new faculty concerns. These questions should be addressed in the first few weeks of employment in order to allow new faculty to be as prepared as possible as they embark on their chosen profession.

- What resources does the institution have to help me get settled? What institutional publications should I have? What mailing lists and/or listservs should I be on to receive information about events, meetings, academic calendars, etc.?

- How important are grants? How do I get hooked into the grant-writing process? Who can help me find out where to meet people to write the best proposal, draw up a budget, receive approval for human subjects?

- How can I gain the type of exposure necessary for good tenure letters?

- Should I put graduate students' names on my papers or articles? In what order? How important is first authorship for promotion and tenure? How is the alphabetical listing of authors viewed?

- How is collaborative work considered for tenure? Is collaborative work encouraged or discouraged? With other members of the department? With colleagues who are more senior or better known? With junior colleagues or graduate students? How important is it to have singly authored papers?

- Should I give talks at other universities or sites? How often? Where? How important is this? How do you get invited to give such talks?

- How do I go about finding people to write references? How many will I need? Does it matter if they are solicited by me? Do unsolicited letters of commendation count?

- How can I get feedback on my performance? When will I be reviewed? What is the process? What do I need to demonstrate for raises, promotion, and tenure?

- What types of raises are typical? When will I find out about my raise?

- What are the policies for family and personal leave? How does my benefits package work?

- What are the campus traditions that I should be aware of? What is the institution's history?

A comprehensive orientation program depends upon good communication. Such a program will answer the critical questions that junior faculty should ask but often fail to ask because they do not have a good understanding of how the academy works. Sometimes questions are not asked because of embarrassment: The new faculty member may be hesitant to look ignorant or unprepared in the eyes of the department chair and may feel that as a faculty member, such information should be understood. Sometimes questions are not addressed because the new professor simply does not know what questions to ask or because she cannot formulate her concerns and anxieties into pertinent, specific questions. By providing answers to typical questions, the chair cannot only inform new faculty members, but may also help them avoid embarrassment or ignorance. How a department chooses to address these issues will depend upon its size and culture; however, both formal and informal orientations can work together to prepare a new faculty member in those first few crucial weeks.

Formal Versus Informal Orientations

Many of these critical questions can be addressed in a formal session in which all new employees participate; moreover, there are issues specifically geared toward tenure-track faculty that should be addressed from an institutional level. An effective orientation plan should consist of both formal and informal ways to impart information and should not start and stop within the first weeks of a given term. However, early, formal orientations are an effective way in which to transmit information that is needed quickly, including human resources information on benefits (retirement and savings plans, insurance options and medical coverage, and so forth) and any departmental and institutional information that a new faculty must know in order to begin the semester.

The above questions may be addressed in a formal or informal orientation; no matter how these questions are answered, it is important to be as honest and open as possible with new faculty members. If there is a departmental or institutional minefield to be negotiated, the caring chair will explain that problem to the new person rather than letting him stumble upon it himself. The key to answering these questions is not simply by handing the new faculty member books and pamphlets outlining institutional policies and procedures, but in working through both the written and unwritten issues surrounding these various questions.

In the vignette that follows, we depict the typical way in which institutions conduct a formal orientation for new faculty. New faculty tend to find the personnel and benefits information important but do not find the orientation very useful as preparation for their new role as a member of a specific department and faculty community.

Scenario: Sarah arrives at her campus orientation eager to find out what being a faculty member at this institution is really like. She chooses a seat and spends the next three hours filling out forms and learning about retirement funds and credit unions. As she leaves clutching a pile of financial information and her still-warm faculty ID, she feels even more uncertain of her new role than when she sat down.

Response: While the forms Sarah fills out are important, this type of institutional orientation does not provide the early connection to the department that she seeks, nor does it answer those critical departmental questions. In fact, these sessions are not true orientations; they are information sessions that do little to help guide the new faculty member at the beginning of a new career. Orientations that deluge new faculty with information in the first day of their appointment, or even in the first couple of weeks, are minimally effective. A year-long program allows faculty to learn more about teaching, service, research, promotion, and tenure while they are actively immersed in the process. In the next part, we will discuss ways in which to design your orientation so that it continues throughout the first year.

Orientation sessions should familiarize newcomers with the criteria, many of which may be unspoken, that will be applied to judge whether the newcomer should be granted promotion and tenure. Many institutions will offer formal orientations to cover the documented policies and leave it to the departments to address the unspoken expectations. Therefore, formal institutional orientations should address accepted expectations and communicate what the institution values. For example, in a liberal arts college where the emphasis is primarily on teaching with minimal expectation for research and publication, orientation sessions should emphasize these priorities. At Hamline University, all new faculty participate in a year-long orientation on how to incorporate writing across the curriculum, one of the distinctive features of their undergraduate curriculum. Whereas Hamline's year-long orientation focuses on teaching, a large department at a major research university could devote a significant aspect of the departmental orientation program to the expectations for research and scholarship, including the facilitators and inhibitors of productivity.

As part of the institutional orientation, new faculty should be introduced to the governance structure of the institution and the department, the chairs of key committees, and key staff and their offices in the institution. The following scenario illustrates a typical problem encountered by many new faculty members.

Scenario: Dan has been on campus for three weeks. Classes are going pretty well, and he has already met with a few students one-on-one. So far, so good in terms of teaching. The major problem now is learning more about the campus—where things are and who is whom. As a graduate student, he was not involved in committee work or in departmental service, so he doesn't even know what he needs to ask about, but he feels disconnected and uncertain about how the college works and how decisions are made.

Response: Provide a road map of who is whom in the department, college, and institution and assign a contact person to show the new hire around, introduce him or her to people in the building and college, and be a point person for general questions. Demonstrate institutional web sites or hand out informational brochures that provide information on faculty, offices, and resources.

Dan clearly did not have a successful orientation to his new institution. He remains adrift without a clear understanding of the institutional structure or governance. Although formal institutional orientations are often organized by the human resources department, an involved chair should be aware of what information is handled at those sessions. Questions that are not addressed will fall to the chair to answer—perhaps in an informal way with faculty one-on-one.

LEGAL ISSUES

The formal institutional orientation should include information that new faculty require in order to be good campus citizens. Legal issues are becoming increasingly important on America's campuses, and new faculty should be made aware of the institution's response to legalities such as the Americans with Disabilities Act, Section 504 of the 1973 Rehabilitation Act, the Buckley Amendment (also known as the Family Educational Rights and Privacy Act of 1974—FERPA), copyright laws for classroom use, and sexual harassment. Campus legal issues such as institutional polices regarding plagiarism and academic dishonesty, the campus judicial process, policies on alcohol, liability coverage in the classroom and off campus for field trips, the academic probation policies, perspectives on sexual harassment, and what information is required for the syllabus should also be covered in this orientation. Institutions with honor or behavioral codes should also lay out these rules. Many of these laws and policies will be covered in the catalog or faculty and student handbooks. Copies of these publications should be made available for new hires, and the pertinent information delivered in a formal orientation to ascertain that new faculty are aware of these issues. The following scenario illustrates problems that can occur when an institution assumes that new faculty members understand legal issues.

Scenario: Veronica receives a call from an irate parent whose son is failing her introductory course. The parent demands to know his son's grades, so Veronica obliges. The parent then tells her that his son has a learning disability and should receive longer time on his tests. He threatens to name her in a lawsuit claiming she has refused to accommodate his son under the ADA. Panicked, Veronica promises that the student may make up his tests and may take as long as he wants.

Response: Not only did Veronica violate the Buckley Amendment by giving a student's grades out over the phone, but she also agreed to make academic accommodations for a student without checking on institutional policy. This sticky legal situation could be averted by providing new faculty with the appropriate legal information that could affect them as professors and advisors.

Many new faculty members will be faced with unfamiliar situations at the beginning of their career, such as an irate call from a parent. The faculty member in the scenario, however, was not prepared to handle these legal issues. An orientation program that illustrates typical scenarios and the appropriate responses would help new faculty members understand the intricacies of legalities affecting postsecondary institutions. Such an orientation could rely on the disabilities office, the registrar's office, and the legal counsel to provide information. Most institutions have procedures for dispensing information about a student and for making accommodations, but such information is not always accessible or even available in the faculty handbook.

One good source for information on national legal issues is the Council on Law in Higher Education (CLHE). This council suggests that institutions have widely available written policies covering FERPA; they also suggest that videotapes and workshops can help to disseminate this information. While professors may understand that students' grades should be kept confidential, they may not know that such items as email, handwriting, videotapes, and audiotapes also may be considered educational records that fall under the Buckley Amendment. CLHE recommends that the following questions be answered in a training session on institutional legalities: What is a school official at your institution? What is directory information at your institution? What is a legitimate educational interest? What are your policies on access to the computer network? (Baskt, 1999).

Another area where legal concerns can arise is sexual harassment. Sexual harassment is prohibited by the amended Title VII of the Civil Rights Act of 1964, Title IX of the Education Amendments of 1972, and at the state level by statute. In addition, most campuses have policies that prohibit the sexual harassment of students, staff, and faculty. Orientation needs to cover appropriate responses to harassment for both faculty and students so that new faculty can respond to incidences of harassment they may personally experience and can direct students to appropriate action if they are harassed.

New faculty orientation sessions need to answer the following questions about sexual harassment: What is it? What can I do if harassment occurs? Whom do I contact? Answering these questions can help avoid incidents like the following.

Scenario: Julie, a new faculty member, has developed a mentoring relationship with Michael, a senior faculty member in the college. Michael, a proficient grantsman, has agreed to coauthor a grant with Julie. In the course of their meetings, Michael indicates he is attracted to Julie. She is not interested and says so. He repeatedly invites her to go out after work, but she declines and says that he is making her uncomfortable. He persists. When the grant is due, he refuses to submit it in spite of Julie's hard work. He tells her that when she goes out with him, the grant can go forward. He also reminds her that he is on the college promotion and tenure committee.

Response: Provide information at orientation that lets faculty members know what to do in the event of a harassing situation (real or perceived). Most campuses have a person designated as a *confidential* contact in the event of such incidents, and faculty need to know campus protocol for what to do and where to go if harassment occurs. Faculty need information that allows them to get the help they need in a nonthreatening way.

The goal of the institutional orientation on legalities is to make certain that faculty are informed employees of the institution and have the information or resources they need in order to answer questions as they arise.

CHECKLIST: INSTITUTIONAL ORIENTATIONS

☐ Introduce faculty to who is whom on campus.

☐ Examine employee benefits, including insurance, retirement, health care, and raises.

☐ Explain campus, state, and federal laws and policies and where to go to have additional questions answered, or to whom to refer students and parents.

☐ Provide institutional guidelines for tenure and promotion, including performance reviews and recommendations.

☐ Offer information on institutional programs for professional development such as grant writing, local conferences, colloquia or other avenues of presentation, listservs, and newsletters.

☐ Communicate institutional values, mission, history, and traditions.

REFERENCE

Bakst, D. (1999). *Student privacy on campus.* Washington, DC: Council on Law in Higher Education.

CHAPTER 6

PLANNING AN EFFECTIVE DEPARTMENTAL ORIENTATION

As part of our preparation as tenure-track faculty, the department chair arranged for the provost to give a talk to the entire department to describe the university's expectations of the review process. It was good to see everyone together and to all get the same information. Judging from the questions and comments, I think even some people at the final stage learned something new.

Boy, do I feel like an idiot. I've been around campus for six weeks now and I still am having difficulty finding my way around and meeting people. The campus is huge, and all the students commute. Some faculty are on campus only in the evenings, so I haven't had the chance to meet them. I know it will take time, but I wish I could at least be introduced to some key people like other department chairs and faculty in the college. Actually, now that I'm talking about it, it would even be nice to meet the rest of the people in the department.

The first days on a new job can be daunting ones. New faculty members are likely to find themselves in a new town, on a new campus, and with an array of new colleagues. The department chair can play a crucial role—both formally and informally—in orienting new faculty to the campus and the department. Ideally, the orientation program should engage faculty in dialogue with their colleagues and with the department chair about the promotion and tenure process. Unfortunately, orientations for new faculty, though they vary in length, content, and purpose, often turn into perfunctory descriptions of bureaucratic procedures with an emphasis on giving basic information about services, benefits, facilities, who is whom in the organization chart, etc. While this kind of information is necessary and useful, it does little to introduce the newcomer to the practices of becoming a connected and productive member of the department and institution.

As discussed in the previous chapter, institutional orientations tend to be rather formal and designed for all new employees, not just new faculty members, so at the departmental level, it is important to fill in any gaps left by the institutional orientation. Formal orientation at the departmental level may include meetings with other faculty members and deans, a packet of information detailing places to go for help with teaching problems or to obtain grant information, written guidelines on the promotion and tenure process, the faculty handbook, and the assignment of a mentor. Informal orientation may include professional social gatherings, regular departmental topic-driven brown bags, regular lunches, or happy hours with department colleagues and spouses, and the occasional impromptu chat with new faculty members. Chairs should attempt to encourage both formal and informal orientations for new faculty because each kind of orientation provides different ways in which to acclimate a new colleague.

Because the newcomer's success is predicated on how well he or she fits into the culture of the department and meets the expectations of academic excellence as defined within the department as well as the institution, the focus of the formal orientation should be on assisting new faculty to develop an understanding of the department's and institution's culture and expectations. This is not to say that the purpose of the orientation is to force conformity, but rather to make sure that if the newcomer violates unspoken rules, he or she will do so knowingly, not accidentally.

The previous chapter discussed the importance of communicating to faculty the answers to institutional questions during their first few weeks at a new institution. In this chapter we will discuss orientation more as a departmental process than a structure. Our emphasis will be on the need to provide basic information that every faculty member should have as well as to create opportunities for newcomers to develop the networks, learn the rules, and acquire the habits that will help them manage their careers and meet their responsibilities to the institution. We will not provide detailed models for structuring orientations. For ideas on creating an orientation structure based on faculty development, see the POD Network web site at http://www.podnetwork.org, or the web site for the University of Kansas's Center for Teaching Excellence at http://eagle.cc.ukans .edu/~cte/OtherSites.html.

CRITICAL QUESTIONS TO BE ANSWERED BY THE DEPARTMENT

The following questions address specific departmental issues and concerns. Providing new faculty with answers to these questions within the first few weeks of employment will make for a smoother transition.

- Who are good contact people I can go to with questions or problems?

- How is lab space allocated? How is equipment maintenance paid for? How is equipment/software/hardware updated? Who provides service for computers?

- Who is the department administrative officer? What is his or her responsibility? How is the department organized? How are decisions made? How do you get things done in the department?

- What can I expect from the support staff? What are the jobs of the support staff and the departmental personnel?

- Is it worthwhile to prepare technical reports and send them to colleagues elsewhere?

- Should I give talks within the department? How often? How should I publicize my work within the department?

- What conferences should I go to? Do I need to have papers accepted to go? How much travel is allowed/expected/demanded? Is it better to go to large conferences or smaller workshops?

- Where should I publish? What should I publish? How much? How often? Are there quantity/quality standards for promotion? How do journals, chapters in edited collections, and conference presentations compare? Should I write or edit a book? A special issue?

- How visible should I be in the department? How is working at home viewed?

- Is there a lunch room or break room near my office with a refrigerator and microwave that I might use? Where do I receive my mail, and how do I mail things from the department?

FORMAL DEPARTMENTAL ORIENTATION

Structuring your orientation into a year-long series of sessions allows you to create several formal occasions for providing information and faculty development (see the outline for year-long orientation at the end of Part III). The department should be aware of what is done at the institutional level and be prepared to answer any of the critical questions not addressed by the institutional orientation.

Robert Boice (1992) describes the ideal first-time orientation session as having the following elements: 1) keep it informal and relaxed, 2) limit the number of administrators to a few and have them make very brief comments, preferably after lunch, 3) organize small clusters of assistant professors, preferably with shared interests, and assign an advanced and exemplary assistant professor to be the facilitator of an informal discussion, 4) offer three 12-minute workshops on teaching, obtaining internal grants, and being a productive scholar. These workshops will serve as a preview of lengthier workshops to be held in subsequent orientation sessions for the year-long orientation process.

Administrative Information

Formal orientations at the department level can aid in creating a cohesive cohort for the new faculty. This cohort may act as a support system for each other as they negotiate their new positions together. For departments that are small and only typically bring in one new faculty member at a time, orientations in the form of one-on-one meetings with the chair or other department members may be planned to transmit crucial information. The following scenario illustrates a problem that may arise if pertinent information is not communicated to the new hire.

Scenario: As Gina tries to put her life on campus in order, she runs into unforeseen bureaucratic problems and feels frustrated in not knowing who might be the best person to resolve them. Her office computer refuses to accept her disks from home, her syllabus is incomplete for her first class because there is no one to type it, and she has a grant proposal that must be signed by a college administrator. She doesn't know the appropriate people to approach to resolve these issues.

Response: Provide a list of typical beginning-of-the-semester problems and who should be contacted. Telling new personnel who does what

in the department gives new faculty a sense of personal ownership for solving such problems and offers them an excellent way
to understand the inner workings of the department. In small
departments, problems such as Gina's can probably be taken
care of by the chair or the secretary, but in large institutions
where the department may be 40 or more professors, it is important for new faculty to know whom to go to before they have a
problem.

Because of their experience in academia and at their institution, many
chairs do not realize how at sea new faculty often are when it comes to
administrative knowledge. Understanding who might take offense if asked
to do someone else's work, who is responsible for certain tasks, and where
to go to have all of one's questions answered can greatly alleviate some awk-
ward moments for new employees.

Promotion and Tenure Concerns

*I had completely forgotten that my dossier had to be ready so
soon. I vaguely remember looking at the directions and that
I had to organize all of my work in a three-ring binder. God,
how am I going to have time to find all the stuff I will need?
I can't remember where I put my teaching evaluations and
my CV has not been updated since I came here. Maybe if I
look at someone else's dossier I can figure out what to do.*

As we have mentioned elsewhere in this handbook, the one theme that
recurs throughout the research on junior faculty is the stress associated
with ambiguous guidelines for promotion and tenure. This is a concern
from a personal standpoint for the particular faculty member, but also
from an institutional standpoint in terms of productivity and effective
contributions. The faculty member who is operating under inordinate
amounts of stress associated with uncertainty about evaluation is not likely
to do his or her best work. Based on years of experience as both a practi-
tioner and researcher, Mary Deane Sorcinelli (e.g., 1989, 1992, 1994,
1999) emphasizes the importance of evaluation for promotion and tenure
that is formative and supportive, especially in the early years on the tenure
track. Establishing rapport relative to the evaluation process can help new
faculty members and their department chairs to converse more easily about
expectations, outcomes, and the evaluation process itself.

For legal reasons many department chairs are reluctant to provide faculty with a "recipe" for tenure, particularly so because criteria often change as a result of new academic priorities. Nevertheless, chairs and senior faculty can provide specific information on what constitutes evidence of academic merit and make the criteria less ambiguous. Chairs can also recommend resources that new faculty might find helpful, such as Robert Diamond's book, *Preparing for Promotion and Tenure Review: A Faculty Guide* (1995) and Peter Seldin's books, *The Teaching Portfolio: A Practical Guide to Improved Performance and Promotion/Tenure Decisions* (1997) and *Changing Practices in Evaluating Teaching* (1999).

One way that department chairs can aid faculty in their promotion and tenure process is by providing a rationale for evaluation guidelines. The promotion and tenure of junior faculty is not solely the responsibility of the individual faculty member seeking advancement; it is the collective responsibility of the department (Wergin, 1994, 1999). In his work on faculty roles and rewards, Wergin urges departments to rethink faculty rewards, keeping in mind departmental mission and the collective good of the department. As junior faculty seek to decode departmental standards for evaluation, department chairs need to make links between departmental mission and activities and departmental rewards. Providing this type of rationale for faculty as they grapple with promotion and tenure will help them see the big picture and how their work fits into the overall mission of the department and the institution.

Some institutions provide specific guidelines for promotion and tenure, but many others do not. The following scenario underscores the confusion that often surrounds the issue of tenure and promotion. This confusion can be traced back to a lack of communication between the decision-makers and the new faculty.

Scenario: Anita asks her officemate, who is in her second year, what she thinks is necessary to get tenure. "Oh, three or four articles, decent teaching evaluations, and lots of service," she replies. Anita's teaching mentor, a faculty member with 20 years of service to the institution, tells her that excellent teaching evaluations are her top priority, followed by numerous conference presentations, a couple of well-placed articles, and consistent service. A fellow researcher explains that a book and several articles, several conference presentations, average teaching evaluations, and minimal service will get her tenure. Anita is left still asking the same question, "What are the expectations for tenure here?"

Response: Provide a step-by-step guide delineating the tenure process at the department and institutional levels. Be clear as to the kinds of activities that new faculty should be spending their time on. If what counts are publications in specific types of journals, assistant professors should be told. And if assistant professors are spending time on activities that the chair knows will not enhance their record in the eyes of the tenure and promotion committee, the chair should alert the faculty member. If the department has a strategic plan with specific goals for research productivity, it is imperative that newcomers be informed.

An example of the kind of specificity that a chair may provide can be found by looking at the department of political science at the University of Arizona. This department has a menu of "prestigious research activities" with very specific publication goals. For example, one of the goals states, "Seventy-five percent of the department's faculty will complete two of the following in the next five-year period." And the options provided include 1) an article in a major disciplinary journal (*American Political Science Review, Journal of Politics,* or *American Journal of Political Science*); (2) an article in a major, specialized subfield, interdisciplinary, or related disciplinary journal; 3) a research book published by major academic or commercial press and favorably reviewed in a major source (i.e., major disciplinary journal, *New York Times,* etc.); and 4) editorship of a major academic journal.

The type of information provided by the University of Arizona's department of political science may seem too much like a recipe for tenure for some departments, particularly for teaching-oriented institutions. But what we want to underscore is that this department has assured that its faculty knows the expectations for promotion and tenure; this kind of specific communication can eliminate surprises and hurt feelings down the road. If your department develops such guidelines, however, it is important to adhere to what has been specified.

Another means to offer specificity and clarity to promotion expectations is to have junior faculty, with support of their department chair, a mentor, and/or a committee, determine goals and objectives for tenure that are tied to the candidate's expertise, departmental needs, and institutional mission. Chait (1998) refers to this process as "tenure by objective." While traditional approaches to tenure call for faculty to meet objectives that are often ambiguous, what "tenure by objective" calls for is a clear delineation of the type and proportion of work the faculty member will accomplish to achieve tenure. When reviewed for tenure under this sort of system, the junior faculty member is not likely to encounter the surprises and uncertainty that are so stressful and counterproductive on the traditional tenure track. Chait points out that this process would "allay concerns among junior faculty about sudden, random, and even antithetical shifts in the expectations of their department's senior faculty and chair" (p. 7).

Preparing the Dossier

A chair may begin guiding the new faculty member through the tenure track process by establishing in the department orientation how to begin collecting information for the promotion and tenure dossier. Preparing the dossier for review need not turn into a dreaded and exhausting experience, yet for many assistant professors the prospect of gathering and organizing their materials causes a great deal of anxiety and procrastination. The following scenario offers a means to avoid this response.

Scenario: It is the beginning of the academic year and Justin, an assistant professor starting the third year on the tenure track, is scheduled to have his mid-probationary review in January. The chair has informed him that he must have his dossier ready for the committee's review by December 1. The chair reminds Justin that he had been given the instructions on how to prepare his dossier several months earlier and emphasizes the importance of following the directions. He also tells Justin that the committee pays a lot of attention to the narrative statement because it tells the committee not only what he has accomplished but also what he is likely to accomplish in the future.

Response: Chairs can help assistant professors develop a system at the start of the probationary review so that archiving information (e.g., presentations made at conferences, student evaluations of teaching, etc.) will be done on an ongoing basis, and when the time comes for putting the dossier together, the major task will be one of arrangement. The goal should be to avoid having to madly search through boxes, drawers, and files for the documentation.

Not surprisingly, newly appointed professors find it hard to think ahead to the next two or four or six years and organize their lives accordingly. They don't realize that time in academia tends to go very fast, and as other priorities become more urgent, it gets harder and harder to create systems of organization. When the time comes for preparing the dossier for mid-probationary review, the first impulse may be to put it off or ask for an extension to get everything organized.

One of our research sites uses a "rainbow" file system for dossier materials (i.e., teaching, research, and service activities are presented in different colored files). Organizing one's accomplishments in files that correspond to the university's categories for review is an easy, effective way for faculty to catalog their activities. Many campuses have very specific formats for how to present accomplishments for promotion and tenure reviews. Chairs should encourage faculty to record their accomplishments using this format, so collating materials at review time is simply a matter of cutting and pasting rather than searching for missing materials. The less time that has to be dedicated to this aspect of the dossier, the more time that the professor can dedicate to crafting the statement of accomplishments, having colleagues review it, and following suggestions for revisions.

One way to ease this dossier crunch is to involve seasoned faculty in departmental orientations, where new and experienced faculty can discuss ways to avoid being overwhelmed by this task, as well as methods to continually update one's portfolio. During an orientation, new faculty might be shown sample dossiers, while newly promoted faculty talk about the process of compiling a promotion file. Alternatively, the newly promoted faculty might discuss, "If I had to do it all over again, what would I do differently?" and "What would I do the same?" Such information should form a basis of the year-long orientation.

It is also a good practice to provide new faculty with a timetable indicating the starting and ending dates for all the performance review stages leading up to the final review for promotion and tenure. The chair should review the timetable once a year with the new faculty member, preferably in conjunction with the annual performance review that institutions typically hold in the spring. This practice assures that communication remains open and the new faculty member knows what goals to set for each year. Beginning such goal-setting at the initial orientation stage is not too soon; after all, the tenure clock has already begun to tick.

INFORMAL ORIENTATION

I received a handbook at the campus orientation for new faculty. After reading it you're supposed to understand what your goals are for the next six years. That's a big assumption, though. Certainly the words are there, but you don't know how those words get translated into policy. In reality, orientation does nothing to change the fact that the whole evaluation process is a mystery.

Just as student success and retention on campus call for involvement in both in- and out-of-class experiences, so too a successful faculty member must be involved on campus and in the profession. However, it is not sufficient to advise faculty to get involved or to network. First, assistant professors may not always know what types of involvement may be beneficial to them and second, they may not know how to initiate the relationships that lead to involvement. The purpose of informal orientation is to create opportunities that will help the new professor become acculturated into the life of the department and institution and to feel less like an outsider. Whereas formal orientation may take place at the institutional or departmental level, informal orientation activities are predominantly in the purview of the department chair.

Earlier we discussed the procedural aspects of promotion and tenure that are likely to be handled through formal orientations. Of equal, or greater, importance is creating opportunities where newcomers get to talk with senior faculty, more informally, about the unwritten aspects of the promotion and tenure process. The following scenario demonstrates the necessity for combining formal and informal orientations at the departmental level.

Scenario: Noah, wanting to do everything by the book, faithfully studies his faculty handbook for information about preparing for promotion and tenure. However, even though the faculty handbook, which is more than ten years old, provides general information on the formal rules, it does not cover the unwritten rules that have emerged over time as the institution's priorities have changed.

Response: Recognize the inherently political nature of the promotion and tenure process and the power structures that surround it and find ways of communicating this knowledge to the new members of the faculty. Be willing to articulate the unwritten rules and informal decision-making networks within the power structure in an informal orientation process.

Examples of the kind of information suited to informal orientation include explaining the difficult personalities and prejudices in the department and institution, relating stories of recent tenure decisions, and helping the new faculty member read between the lines of the stated policies. For example, if the provost or president is very concerned with traditional measures of research excellence, then it is important to explain how those priorities influence the review process.

It is also important to help assistant professors differentiate between symbolic goals that are articulated by academic leaders and actual goals. A few years ago, research universities made a big push to give teaching greater weight in the evaluation process, yet for the most part promotion and tenure continue to be primarily determined by the quality and quantity of scholarly accomplishments. Likewise, new faculty who are used to the "publish or perish" model might not understand the real value and importance placed on service at a small liberal arts college and so might eschew such responsibilities.

Professional Affiliations and Networking

I had been trying to write a paper based on my dissertation, but it just did not seem like what I had come up with was good enough to present at a national meeting. Besides, I did not think that I could put a proposal together in such a short time, and I did not want to submit something that I did not feel proud of and sure that it would get accepted.

An assistant professor's academic capital is enhanced by participation in prestigious professional groups—for example, in psychology the relevant group is the American Psychological Association (APA), in sociology it is the American Sociological Association (ASA), in English it is the Modern Language Association (MLA), and so on—as well as by their level of involvement—being elected to an office, being asked to review research proposals for the annual program, appearing in the program as a presenter or in a more minor role such as session chair or discussant. The newcomer's integration into these networks depends on attending the conferences and making themselves known to the more senior people. Some assistant professors may have established their connections to the profession while they were graduate students and will know what they must do to maintain them. But there are also many professors who, like Karen in the scenario that follows, will benefit from the sponsorship of established faculty.

Scenario: At the beginning of her first semester at Middle America University, Karen sees the call for proposals to present research papers at the next meeting of the American Sociological Association. She has attended the meeting as a graduate student, but she has never presented a paper and has heard that it is very difficult to get one accepted. She decides she is not ready to present her research on resilience among homeless school children.

Response: Chairs can facilitate the newcomer's entry by stressing the importance of attending the professional meetings of their discipline on an annual basis, providing travel support, and sharing announcements inviting proposals for research panels and symposia. The most effective way of integrating the newcomer is by inclusion in panel presentations planned by senior faculty who are well established and know the ins and outs of getting into the programs.

As a senior faculty member, the chair may introduce new faculty not only to the institutional culture, but to the professional world as well. In this respect, the chair may pick up where the dissertation advisor left off. Although new faculty have been in the field for some time doing graduate work, making those vital networking connections may not always come easily to newcomers, particularly those who tend towards introversion. Making those professional connections easier—by nominating new faculty to serve on committees of regional and national organizations, providing funding to attend conferences, encouraging and valuing collaborative research, and introducing them to visiting scholars and speakers—will ultimately benefit the department and the field as well as the individual faculty member.

Making the Connection

In addition to providing networking opportunities for new faculty during their first weeks on campus, the caring chair will also help foster a connection to colleagues and the institution. Making a new colleague feel welcomed on a personal level as well as mentored on a professional level can help assure that the new faculty member will begin to form an attachment to the institution. Ways to foster this attachment include how the new faculty member is introduced to the department community and how social interactions are engineered. Early introductions to staff members and new faculty should include more information than just the person's name and specialty. By finding out a few personal details from a new person, or by including familiar topics in the introduction, a chair can help a new faculty member feel valued. Where did the new faculty member grow up? What does he or she like to do outside of work? Has the new faculty member's family come to the new location? Such questions begin to form a bond on a personal level. It is also important for the chair to share his or her nonacademic interests as well. This kind of sharing can make an administrator seem more inviting and can signal that it is acceptable to have interests beyond the job. Providing some personal information during introductions can also help new faculty find people in the institution with similar interests.

CHECKLIST: DEPARTMENTAL ORIENTATIONS

☐ Provide information on department personnel and their responsibilities as well as the department's organization and committees.

☐ Discuss practical information on the requirements for promotion and tenure.

☐ Demonstrate how to collect and maintain tenure-related documentation that is up to date and catalogued in an organized dossier.

☐ Help new faculty understand the politics of promotion and tenure.

☐ Sponsor the participation of new faculty in professional activities and organizations.

REFERENCES

Boice, R. (1992). *The new faculty member: Supporting and fostering professional development.* San Francisco, CA: Jossey-Bass.

Chait, R. (1998). *Ideas in incubation: Three possible modifications to traditional tenure procedures.* Washington, DC: AAHE.

Diamond, R. M. (1995). *Preparing for promotion and tenure review: A faculty guide.* Bolton, MA: Anker.

Seldin, P. (1997). *The teaching portfolio: A practical guide to improved performance and promotion/tenure decisions* (2nd ed.). Bolton, MA: Anker.

Seldin, P. (1999). *Changing practices in evaluating teaching: A practical guide to improved faculty performance and promotion/tenure decisions.* Bolton, MA: Anker.

Sorcinelli, M. D. (1989). Chairs and the development of new faculty. *The Department Advisor 5* (2), 1-4.

Sorcinelli, M. D. (1992). New and junior faculty stress: Research and responses. In M. D. Sorcinelli & A. E. Austin (Eds.), *Developing new and junior faculty* (pp. 27-37). San Francisco, CA: Jossey-Bass.

Sorcinelli, M. D. (1994). Effective approaches to new faculty development. *Journal of Counseling Development, 72,* 474-487.

Sorcinelli, M. D. (1999, Summer). New pathways II: The tenure process. *The Department Chair, 10* (1), 3-4.

Wergin, J. F. (1994). *The collaborative department: How five campuses are inching toward cultures of collective responsibility.* Washington, DC: AAHE.

Wergin, J. F. (1999, Spring). New pathways II: The changing academic climate. *The Department Chair, 9* (4), 3-4.

CHAPTER 7

ORIENTING NEW FACULTY
TO TEACHING

My first day of class was very interesting. The classroom I was assigned to for my introductory course seats about 30 people, and there are 75 students signed up for my class. This is the kind of thing that is hard when you are new. Who do you ask to fix this type of situation? The secretary was swamped with drop and add, so it took her a long time to deal with my problem. I wish I knew who to call for these types of things.

I got a letter from the faculty personnel committee saying "We hope that you make yourself available to students." So I had to respond. I showed them that I had set aside six hours a week for office hours and that I gave students my home phone number as well as my office number.

While many institutions—particularly large, research-oriented universities—offer extensive teaching orientation to new graduate students, few provide the same benefits for tenure-track faculty. Since many disciplines do not allow graduate students to be fully responsible for courses, many newly minted PhDs may arrive at their first tenure-track jobs with little or no teaching experience. Fink (1992) notes that approximately 50% of new faculty arrive at their first tenure-track job without having had full responsibility for a course. Suddenly they are expected to choose books, write syllabi, and plan courses and lectures without any pedagogical background or understanding of educational theory. Baldwin

(1990) notes that "developing effective teaching skills is perhaps the most immediate concern of the new professor" (p. 32). Orientations geared toward answering teaching questions and preparing new professors to be successful teachers can ease stress caused by inexperience and can help assure that new professors know how to tackle this aspect of their chosen profession.

Teaching orientations should cover practical aspects of instruction at your institution, provide models for courses and syllabi, and discuss issues that are likely to arise in the classroom or during office hours. Not only can teaching orientations introduce new faculty to their instructional responsibilities, but such programs provide an avenue for sharing good practices and enhancing the teaching of all professors in the department.

CRITICAL QUESTIONS CONCERNING TEACHING

The following are essential questions that need to be addressed in order for new faculty to feel informed and prepared for their new teaching position.

- Which are good courses to teach? It is good to teach service subjects, or bad, or indifferent? Is it good to teach the same course, or stay within a single area, or teach around?

- Is it a good thing to develop a new course? An undergraduate course? A specialized course in my research area?

- How do I get a teaching assistant?

- Are there departmental or institutional guidelines for grading? What is the grading system? Are any courses taken pass/fail? How are grades reported? When?

- How do I request what courses and at what times I'd like to teach in a given semester?

- How many office hours a week are expected?

- What resources are available on campus to help me with my teaching? Who has taught my assigned classes in the past? Where are sample syllabi located?

- How are examination and desk copies ordered? Where do I place book orders for my classes? How do I place books on reserve in the library? How do I go about requesting that the library buy resource materials?

TEACHING MENTORS

As part of the formal orientation, new faculty should be given an introduction to the major teaching policies of the institution such as deadlines for submitting final grades, procedures in the case of being unable to meet a class, policies related to the cancellation of classes, teacher-student relationships, institutional guidelines related to harassment, and procedures for dealing with students who violate academic regulations. Additionally, as illustrated below, new faculty need to know how they should deal with the kinds of administrative problems that usually erupt in the first few weeks of the semester.

Scenario: As a graduate assistant, Annabelle was responsible for teaching lab sections of a large chemistry course. Until her first job as an assistant professor, she had never been responsible for an entire course. As a new faculty member, she has two introductory chemistry courses and an upper-level inorganic course to teach. A couple of weeks before the beginning of the semester, she sets out to work on her syllabus, but other than the daily assignments, she has little idea what to include and how to distinguish the information needed for the nonmajor course and that needed for the major course.

Response: Chairs who have provided syllabi from previous courses at that institution will have begun the teaching orientation prior to the new faculty's arrival. But while providing examples of excellence from other teachers is a good start, simply providing samples may not be enough to initiate new professors into the teaching profession. Many new faculty can benefit from mentors who advise them of the different aspects of the transition into faculty life. While a research mentor may be a wonderful researcher who publishes regularly, that person may have little interest in teaching. Providing new faculty with mentors who are also excellent teachers can give new teachers an outlet for questions and ideas.

In some ways, teaching mentors may be even more crucial in the first few weeks than a research mentor. Because new faculty are thrust into new courses and new classrooms with new students when they first arrive, having someone with whom to discuss problems, concerns, or ideas can solve many of the issues that arise before they become insurmountable problems. A teaching mentor that meets weekly with the new faculty member can offer an avenue to discuss day-to-day issues such as how to handle students with attendance problems, what to do when students do not complete assignments on time, how to generate lively discussions, and so on. Department chairs can also facilitate teaching mentoring by encouraging new faculty to seek out other members of the department for advice on various teaching questions. Sometimes a word here and there about an interesting pedagogical approach or a successful class provides the newcomer with a source to tap for good ideas.

FACULTY DEVELOPMENT SERVICES

In addition to assigning teaching mentors, chairs can investigate the services provided on the campus for teaching improvement. Many institutions now have offices or committees devoted to faculty development, and such services can provide a wealth of information for new teachers. Chairs should not only know what the campus has to offer, but should also consider working with such services to create departmental teaching development. Many offices around campus will welcome the opportunity to educate faculty concerning their services and how faculty can best take advantage of all the institution has to offer. The scenario that follows illustrates the value of such an orientation.

Scenario: Sam arrived at his new institution—a small liberal arts college—with syllabi for his new courses in hand. He had prepared them over the summer. Before the semester began, the entire faculty met for two days to have workshops on incorporating service and collaborative learning into courses. This workshop was developed because the institution's mission statement had recently been revised to reflect its new service goals. The directors of internships and community service and the career placement office spoke about service learning opportunities. Based on ideas from his new colleagues and information from a faculty development expert, Sam revised some key assignments to add more collaboration and service learning into his course requirements.

Response: This chair and her colleagues made institutional goals clear to the faculty and then provided ways in which to meet those goals in the curriculum. The message to faculty was clear, and the tools were provided. This institution also provided an excellent way for new faculty to become involved with teaching colleagues from different departments.

Large departments may also consider bringing in outside teaching experts to lead faculty—new and returning—in teaching workshops before the semester begins. Such workshops not only add to faculty development, but also contribute to the departmental bonding process. Small institutions may handle such workshops within a given school or as a whole faculty. Topics might be very specific or more general and might include incorporating service learning into the classroom, using the web for course discussion, involving students in collaborative work, increasing the effectiveness of lectures, teaching in the large lecture setting, responding to students' written work, promoting critical thinking, and so forth. The positive nature of these topics also underscores an important aspect of teaching orientations: Keep it positive. Eble and McKeachie (1986) explain that effective programs heightened the faculty's "sense of worth to the university" and "offered opportunities for the achievers" rather than threatening faculty or increasing their insecurities (pp. 216-217).

In addition to focusing on improving teaching rather than fixing problems, teaching orientations should practice what they preach. An orientation devoted to effective teaching that is taught in a dry or ineffective way will negate the potential positive results it is trying to engender. Orientations should be interactive, informative, and thought provoking. Feedback can help departments continually improve to meet the genuine needs of the faculty.

Not only do faculty development activities centered around teaching promote teaching excellence in your department, but as Donald Jarvis (1991) points out, they also "legitimize teaching as a respectable topic of conversation among serious academics" (p. 56). Institutions that value teaching, reward excellent teaching, and require it for promotion and tenure should openly communicate this to new faculty by providing them with the tools to be good teachers. Having good teachers in the department lead such sessions can also legitimize teaching as a topic for department programs, and faculty ownership of such activities can be key to their success and longevity. Despite a recent focus on improving college teaching, many faculty still view teaching as less important than research and will give it less time. Because of this attitude, departments concerned with improving teaching should make attendance at teaching orientations mandatory (Jarvis, 1991). Some institutions support mandatory programs by offering a stipend to participants.

Southeast Missouri State University has a mandatory week-long teaching workshop before the fall semester for all new faculty (Fink, 1992). New faculty are surveyed before they arrive to give input on topics to be covered and to provide opportunities for them to share their own expertise or good practices. This program includes information about the community and institution, but the main focus is on teaching effectiveness. The first day is an all-day workshop, and the following four days are mandatory for the morning sessions with voluntary afternoon sessions on various topics and activities such as library tours or advising students. The sessions are designed to be interactive, and the workshop itself is presented in a positive way to underscore the priority this institution places on teaching effectiveness.

While faculty development offices and pre-semester teaching workshops can help hone new instructors' teaching skills, it is the responsibility of the department to ensure that new faculty are adequately prepared to teach in the discipline. Ideally, this task should fall on the doctoral institution, but increasingly, new PhDs receive a narrow, specialized education and begin new faculty positions ill-equipped to teach the larger issues of the discipline in an introductory course to the average undergraduate (Jarvis, 1991). Teaching orientations not only ensure that new PhDs are ready to meet the needs of broad-based, introductory courses, but also that the department philosophy is imparted. Many institutions that offer multiple sections of general education or prerequisite courses strive to make the various sections as uniform as possible in order to make certain that students are prepared for the next course in the sequence. Teaching orientations can introduce new faculty to the established goals and breadth of such courses and can illustrate ways in which the new professor can also make the course his or her own.

Early orientations devoted to teaching not only provide valuable information for new faculty but can lead to interpersonal bonding and an early connection to the institution. Since many new faculty leave graduate school unaware of the various pedagogical possibilities available to them in the modern classroom, teaching orientations can introduce them to innovative ways in which to use technology, ideas for increasing critical thinking and incorporating collaborative learning, methods other than lecturing for heavy content-driven courses, etc. Chairs play an integral role in this orientation. If no institutional program exists, the chair may introduce a program into the department; if a centralized program does exist, the chair can encourage the department's new faculty to take advantage of what is offered.

CHECKLIST: TEACHING ORIENTATIONS

☐ Review administrative policies and procedures that are related to teaching.

☐ Make available sample syllabi, course outlines, final exam schedules, and new grade books.

☐ Review grading policies and procedures.

☐ Provide workshops for sharing ideas and frustrations in teaching led by good teachers on the faculty.

☐ Explain how to deal with problems that may arise in the classroom.

☐ Provide a teaching mentor.

☐ Inform new faculty about teaching enhancement resources available on campus such as the faculty development office.

☐ Discuss teaching awards and evaluations and their impact on tenure and promotion decisions.

☐ Run sessions that practice what they preach.

REFERENCES

Baldwin, R. G. (1990). Faculty career stages and implications for professional development. In J. H. Schuster & D. W. Wheeler (Eds.), *Enhancing faculty careers: Strategies for development and renewal* (pp. 20-40). San Francisco, CA: Jossey-Bass.

Boice, R. (1992). *The new faculty member: Supporting and fostering professional development.* San Francisco, CA: Jossey-Bass.

Eble, K., & McKeachie, W. J. (1986). *Improving undergraduate education through faculty development.* San Francisco, CA: Jossey-Bass.

Fink, L. D. (1992). Orientation programs for new faculty. In M. D. Sorcinelli & A. E. Austin (Eds.), *Developing new and junior faculty.* New Directions for Teaching and Learning, No. 50. San Francisco, CA: Jossey-Bass.

Jarvis, D. K. (1991). *Junior faculty development: A handbook.* New York, NY: The Modern Language Association.

Chapter 8

Addressing Service and Campus Community Concerns

I thought I was prepared to hit the ground running as a faculty member. After I earned my master's degree, I was an instructor at a community college for three years, and I also was involved as a teaching and research assistant during my doctoral work. I thought my life was so busy then that I just figured nothing could be busier or more demanding. Well, I was wrong. Here I am just getting started in this position and already I feel totally over my head. I just moved to a new town, I have 20 advisees, I'm teaching three courses that I've never taught before, and I'm trying to get my dissertation published. I'm not complaining, I'm just saying it's not what I expected. I thought I was ready for this, and now that I'm here, I'm just not sure if I am. I hope I can keep up with all of this.

―――・・―――

In the first year I noticed how often women faculty talked about how much they worked. It seemed to have a competitive flavor: "I was up until 2:00 in the morning," "Well, I was up until 3:00 and I'm on 80 committees, and blah, blah, blah." I got the sense that the more overworked you were, the better faculty person you were.

―――・・―――

I tried very hard not to succumb to what felt like a lot of pressure to participate [in committees] from my chair. I'm trying to establish myself as a part of the community here, and if I say, "Wait a minute! The rules say you can't make

> *me do this," what kind of image am I painting of myself?*
> *And, you know, it is important to be accepted by my col-*
> *leagues, and that's quite a bit of pressure.*

Trying to be a good department and campus citizen often means that new faculty feel overwhelmed in their first few weeks and months in a new position. Graduate school and nontenured teaching positions do not prepare new faculty for the time, emotional, and intellectual commitments of committee work and advising. The stress described in the excerpts above is not uncommon for new faculty, or even for seasoned faculty. The department chair can help ease this stress by aiding new professors in setting priorities and understanding the service obligations at their institution. Unfortunately, it is easy for new faculty to say yes to all requests for service in an effort to be involved and to become a team player. The chair can help protect new faculty from becoming too immersed in service and from spreading their time too thin.

CRITICAL QUESTIONS ABOUT SERVICE AND THE CAMPUS COMMUNITY

By addressing the following questions, department chairs can help to alleviate any anxiety new faculty may have about service responsibilities.

- How should my time be divided among teaching, advising, grant writing, committee work and other service, and research?

- How much committee work should I do? Which committees should I turn down if asked to serve? How much time should I expect to spend on committee work? Does it matter if the committee work is within the department? The institution?

- What types of outside service should I do? Paper and proposal reviewing? Journal assistant editorships? Conference organizer?

- What special resources are there for women? For minority faculty?

- What resources are available for faculty who are disabled?

- Is there a dress code or are there expectations for faculty attire or behavior? (A number of private institutions may require faculty to sign a code of conduct or honor, and there may be certain unwritten expectations that go along with such institutional cultures.)

The issues that these questions address concern institutional culture and the campus community. While some of these questions may be answered in the formal orientations discussed in previous chapters, we have placed these questions together because they ask for information on topics that are often neglected in many centralized orientations. Many of these topics lend themselves to informal orientation models because they may be specific to certain groups of faculty or because they touch on sensitive matters like professional attire and physical challenges.

Department chairs should help faculty understand the academic pecking order of service obligations. Many new faculty express a concern about the time committees take away from more serious academic work, but some faculty believe that this work will be taken into consideration at promotion and tenure time. Chairs can express to new faculty how much or little service will contribute to tenure decisions. For institutions without tenure, service or administrative responsibilities may play a larger part in a faculty member's continuing status.

TIME MANAGEMENT

The majority of new faculty struggle with the issue of time management. Chairs can be proscriptive about the amount of time new faculty put into outside commitments by requiring committee chairs to go through the department head when requesting committee assignments for faculty. In this way, chairs can place new faculty on less demanding committees and can limit the service commitments for new hires. The scenario that follows outlines a typical experience for new faculty.

Scenario: Larry is a new faculty member at a state university, and when we talked to him in an interview, he was simply overwhelmed. His new job requires him to teach 21 credits per year; to maintain connections with the discipline through national and regional conferences; to provide service in the local community through professional activities; to be an involved institutional citizen in at least two departmental, college, and university committees; and to maintain some semblance of a research and publication record.

Response: Larry's job responsibilities are fairly typical of a faculty member. If he is to do all he is called to do in his first year (and even the first semester), he will need to learn how to manage his time. His chair could aid him by limiting his committee involvement in the first year and by helping him organize his time through developing priorities.

Two important skills for success in academe are time management and planning. When new hires begin their duties, department chairs can help them establish a plan for what they want to accomplish in their first year. This general plan can be a focal point for the new faculty member to prioritize activities and also for the department chair to see how these activities fit with departmental priorities. At the end of this chapter are two checklists (Time Management and Do's and Don'ts for Orientation Activities) that suggest topics to cover when working with faculty to plan for their future.

If your campus requires teaching, research, and service, then faculty need to establish guidelines to allocate their time. There are some duties from which the new faculty member can obtain release time in the first year. For example, most chairs try to ease new faculty into service. Teaching and research, however, require instant attention even if there is release time involved. Teaching starts the first day of the new semester, and research is constantly demanding. In the previous chapters we discussed ways in which to orient new faculty to professional and teaching obligations in a new institution. We conclude this section with a summary of points covered in an article published in *Academe* by Walter Gmelch titled "It's About Time" (1996, 22–26), in which he describes the tendency of faculty (regardless of rank) to feel constantly overwhelmed by their responsibilities, so much so that it appears impossible that they will ever be able to fulfill all of their commitments.

Gmelch provides several excellent recommendations on how academics can be in control of their time. We suggest that chairs use these recommendations to form the basis of a discussion on time management with new faculty. Gmelch provides the following suggestions:

- Realize that paperwork, meetings, and interruptions represent not the ends of academic productivity but the means to achieving academic goals.

- Reserve at least 20% of your time for focused effort on "high pay-offs" (HIPOS) activities. HIPOS represent the critical three or four make-or-break functions of a faculty member, such as publishing manuscripts, teaching effectively, building positive collegial relations, and providing community service.

- Identify the vital few high pay-off activities that will help you attain excellence in teaching, scholarship, and service.

- Reduce involvement in the trivial, less meaningful, low pay-off (LOPOS) activities by cutting back excessive meetings, unproductive committee work, and general administrivia.

- Arrange your working environment so that telephone calls can be screened, recorded, or forwarded to block off uninterrupted time.

- Find a retreat or HIPO hideout where you can spend uninterrupted time such as a lab, home office, or private space in the library.

Gmelch makes some important distinctions that are critical to better time management. First, he differentiates between efficient versus effective time management, the former as "doing things right" and the latter being "doing the right things." Second, he differentiates between urgent and important tasks. Urgent tasks call for immediate attention (e.g., a ringing telephone, an email message on the screen) and important tasks that rarely need to be done on that day or next week or even next month (e.g., writing a paper for a conference that is eight months away, revising a paper for publication). According to Gmelch, faculty should spend 80% of their time on the important tasks and 20% on the urgent ones, but in reality most do the inverse. Not having clear and purposeful goals, persisting in doing things because they have always done them, and the need to keep busy are some of the reasons why they concentrate on the urgent but not necessarily important tasks.

A sure sign that an assistant professor may be overwhelmed by the urgent is when he/she complains frequently about "not having enough time to do everything," "staying up until dawn to grade papers," or "not having had enough time to submit a proposal to present at a conference." Individuals who are trapped by the urgent seem constantly under stress, and their interactions with others are usually about their sense of over-work, as if it were a badge of courage. Some strategies by which chairs can help assistant professors reduce the time they spend on urgent tasks include advising them to question 1) Why am I doing this? 2) When will I stop doing this? 3) What would happen if I stopped? 4) How does this activity contribute to my goals?

Additionally, chairs can advise assistant professors on strategies to increase the time spent on important tasks, including 1) scheduling daily time for planning, 2) allowing high pay-off activities (e.g., preparing for teaching, writing, developing collegial networks) rather than pressures determine daily activities, 3) identifying low pay-off activities (e.g., serving on an unproductive committee, spending too much time in meetings) and asking "What is this for?", 4) eliminating everything that is no longer productive, and 5) establishing and updating goals to reinforce professional and personal high pay-off activities.

In addition to helping new faculty manage their time, chairs can also help them to balance their time. When we think of time management and academia, most of us conjure images of ways in which to produce more publications and spend more time on teaching plans. However, in order for new faculty to be able to sustain their productivity and health, a balance must be found between work and personal time. New faculty need to know that it is acceptable to take time off to spend with family and friends and to recharge their own batteries. By helping new faculty manage their time, a chair can also disseminate the message about balancing time.

In order to facilitate this message, we recommend that chairs and assistant professors read *The Seven Habits of Highly Effective People: Powerful Lessons in Personal Change* by Stephen R. Covey. While this is the kind of book one might tend to dismiss as another self-help book full of quick recipes that ignore the institutional context, we have found that the strategies suggested for being more productive can be helpful to faculty members who are involved in a variety of fast-paced activities. In particular, the author's discussion of the difference between urgent and important is of great relevance to those of us who are more likely to read and respond to email messages (urgent because they are staring at us) than to schedule time to begin writing a conference paper (important because it contributes to our professional development and tenure portfolio).

The next chapter will focus on activities that continue the orientation process throughout the first year of a faculty member's tenure at an institution.

CHECKLIST: TIME MANAGEMENT

☐ Map out the year ahead to establish priorities and organize time.

☐ Encourage balanced involvement from the start.

☐ Identify high pay-off activities.

☐ Relegate or delegate low pay-off activities.

☐ Focus effort to avoid constant interruptions.

☐ Accomplish similar tasks in a block of time.

☐ Make a schedule and adhere to it.

☐ Create an environment that is conducive to productivity away from ringing phones and chatty neighbors.

☐ Don't be afraid to be selfish with your time.

CHECKLIST: DO'S AND DON'TS FOR ORIENTATION ACTIVITIES

DO

☐ Develop orientation activities throughout the first year.

☐ Provide formal and informal opportunities for orientation.

☐ Make sure faculty have a fair representation of both campus and institutional priorities for success.

☐ Ask new faculty the areas in which they need help (e.g., time management).

☐ Involve both senior and junior faculty in orientation sessions.

DON'T

☐ Assume that new faculty members will ask for the information they need to get started on the tenure track.

☐ Forget to supplement formal information with informal, "insider" information.

☐ Front-load the year with all the orientation opportunities in the first month of the first term.

☐ Assume that a campus-wide orientation will provide the newcomer with all they need to know to get started as a faculty member.

REFERENCES

Covey, S. R. (1995). *The seven habits of highly effective people: Powerful lessons in personal change.* Provo, UT: Covey Leadership Center.

Gmelch, W. H. (1996). It's about time. Academe, 82 (5), 22-26

Chapter 9

FULL-YEAR ORIENTATION PROGRAMS

When I look back on my first year, one word comes to mind—overwhelming. I felt like I was bombarded with information in the first two weeks of the semester, fawned over for being new, and then quickly left out to dry. I was surprised how fast the novelty of my being new wore off for my colleagues. Once school started full swing, I felt like I just went back and forth to class and sat in my office like the rest of the people in my department. I rarely saw any of my colleagues and pretty much spent the rest of the year in a fog. I barely knew what to do with myself.

In our department we do a really neat thing to bring new people together based on common interests. As a faculty we meet twice a month. One meeting is mostly business, and the other briefly covers business and then moves to a topic that is of concern to all of us. Like earlier this year we had two sessions on technology. In the first we just talked about the different ways to use technology in the classroom. A faculty member in our department who uses computers a lot for teaching helped lead the discussion. The second was real hands-on. We went to the college's new technology classroom and got a primer on how to use the equipment. I definitely appreciated these sessions. I also appreciate the concept in general. As the newest person in the department, I relish the opportunity to get together with my colleagues and to focus on things related to teaching and research. It seems like a safe place and an easy time to bring up my concerns.

When I started I felt okay, and things were going well. I felt in control. The isolation didn't really hit me until about November when the novelty of being new wore off and people were doing their own thing. I had the weirdest feeling—I simply didn't know what to do with myself. I had release time, but frankly didn't know what to do with it. Of course, I knew I should be publishing and spending time on my classes, but the knowledge wasn't enough. I felt like I needed a boost or something. It would have been nice to have ongoing support throughout the first year. I felt new all year, not just the first month when everyone seemed to be focused on my "newness."

As we have discussed throughout this book, new faculty development is not a one shot deal, a concept which is illustrated in the first excerpt above. This faculty member experienced a feeling of newness that went on well beyond the first week's orientation activities, but his department did not acknowledge that newness. The second and third excerpts show how important ongoing orientations can be. New faculty development must focus on all aspects of faculty work and take place throughout the first year and beyond. The department chair plays a crucial role in creating a climate for ongoing faculty development and involving all members of the department in fostering new faculty success. Junior faculty development is the primary responsibility of the department chair, but in a functional department, it should involve all faculty.

While orientation at the beginning of the semester is important and necessary to help new faculty start their position, our plan is not to deluge faculty with too much information too quickly. Year-long orientation programs overcome this problem of information overload by providing information in installments and allowing faculty easy access to information as new situations arise.

There is no set model for year-long orientations. For example, at Chico State University, California, all new faculty meet as a group throughout the year to discuss salient issues and to learn more about the university. Early in the year topics include information that is typically covered in an orientation: benefits, getting things done in the university, and administrivia. As the year goes on, faculty discuss issues that are distinctly related to being a new faculty member, such as teaching evaluations, the promotion and tenure process, and applying for grants. The program benefits faculty by providing pertinent information for all faculty members and by offering new faculty time to develop relationships with other faculty on campus. By meeting throughout the year, new faculty members have time to digest information and to forge new friendships.

Another model for extended orientation comes from the Office for Minority Faculty Development (OMFD) at Penn State University. The program, while targeted to support ethnic and cultural minorities, is open to all faculty members and provides a rich resource for the university community. Throughout the year, the OMFD hosts intensive three-hour workshops on topics specifically designed to help the junior faculty member. Topics include grant writing, preparing a dossier, effective teaching, writing for publication, and promotion and tenure. The program, where possible, calls upon senior minority faculty to conduct the workshops. This practice provides role models of success for new faculty, opens the door to mentoring possibilities, and offers experienced perspectives on important issues for the new faculty member. The extended time period is useful, as it allows time for actually doing whatever is covered in the workshop with the watchful support of a seasoned faculty member.

In the absence of campus-wide orientation programs like those just mentioned, there are many things department chairs can do incrementally to give new faculty timely information. Year-long orientation may take the form of monthly departmental meetings dedicated to different topics (as mentioned in the excerpt at the outset of this chapter), bimonthly or monthly meetings led by faculty in the department with particular expertise in a given area, or biannual departmental retreats. Although they can take many forms, extended orientations should include timely topics for new faculty. These topics should include information on tenure (in a general sense), teaching, research, and service—in greater or lesser degrees depending on institutional requirements and cultures.

TEACHING-FOCUSED WORKSHOPS

As mentors, department chairs should introduce new faculty to a variety of teaching issues. Extended orientations are an ideal place to address teaching concerns in that the expanse of time allows faculty the chance to address issues as they experience them. Topics throughout the year should include the campus culture for teaching, student retention, learning styles, teaching styles, new pedagogy, and student evaluations.

In many fields and institutions, teaching is no longer a matter of giving a 50-minute lecture, yet most new faculty members have not been prepared for all that teaching involves. Most new faculty members model and adapt teaching styles they learned from their professors. Consequently, in their first teaching positions, many new faculty find themselves ill-equipped to teach effectively. Teaching anxiety is one of the first stress areas a new faculty member experiences. Year-long workshops to hone teaching skills can help alleviate this anxiety and develop new faculty into successful teachers. Such workshops may be conducted within the department or through an institution's faculty development office.

Teaching orientation sessions might include discussions of different teaching styles and what styles may (or may not) be appropriate for different situations. Pat Hutchings (1996), of the Carnegie Foundation for the Advancement of Teaching, suggests the model of a "teaching circle" whereby meetings are planned for faculty to formally come together for a specified period of time (e.g., the academic year) to discuss teaching and teaching related concerns as they arise. Teaching circles, Hutchings points out, are cheap, easy to plan, and very useful. At the outset, new faculty are likely to benefit from topical discussions of things like syllabi preparation, the institution's grading standards, and using technology in the classroom. This is the type of information faculty can use immediately. Topics later in the semester might include using group work in class, responding to student papers, using portfolios, or involving students in discussions. The teaching circle stands to benefit the entire department by involving all faculty in conversations about teaching and by increasing collegiality and an understanding of each other's pedagogy.

In departments where teaching has been neglected or is in need of new ideas, the hiring of new faculty offers the opportunity to revitalize teaching. A department chair can encourage new thinking about teaching by introducing the newcomer to the burgeoning literature on the pedagogical philosophies and methods of collaborative learning; antiracist, culturally responsive, and feminist teaching approaches; or using technology to enhance learning. As campuses become more racially and ethnically diverse as well as more varied in the age and interests of the student population, professors will be challenged to adopt new approaches and turn their classrooms into learning communities that meet the needs of nontraditional student populations. Most graduate programs have failed miserably at preparing future members of the professoriate to be good teachers, and there is no indication that they are preparing their graduates to teach effectively in the multiracial and multicultural classroom. Department chairs are wise to use orientation meetings for new faculty to introduce these ideas to all faculty in the department.

We close our discussion on teaching with some sound advice from a teaching professional. Success at teaching requires a strong start and ongoing support. We asked Professor Maryellen Weimer, a national expert on teaching and author of *Improving College Teaching: Strategies for Improving Instructional Effectiveness,* "If a chair asked you for advice on how to help a new faculty member with their teaching, what would you say?" Her response provides an excellent and easy-to-implement plan for department chairs to help new faculty and to create a departmental climate that supports good teaching. The references at the end of this chapter include other good teaching resources in addition to the ones that Weimer mentions in her advice.

HELPING NEWCOMERS BECOME GOOD TEACHERS
Professor Maryellen Weimer's Advice to Chairs

I'd begin by visiting them in their offices shortly before the start of the school year. I'd bring with me a modest collection of instructional publications and tell them that I hoped these would be the first of many in their instructional libraries. What resources would I bring? I'm probably not the person to ask since I'm directly involved with some of the publications I'd recommend, but I'd bring an assortment that might include a subscription to a newsletter on teaching—something like *The Teaching Professor* (published by Magna) or *The Forum* (published by ERIC). I'd also bring some books. My favorites for new faculty include Wilbert McKeachie's venerable *Tips for Teachers* (now in its 9th edition), Kenneth Eble's *The Craft of Teaching* (2nd edition), or my own *Improving Your Classroom Teaching* (part of a series published for new faculty by Sage)—you could buy this particular collection for less than $100. Or if being so prescriptive was not my style, I might bring a memo which gave the new faculty person a subscription to the pedagogical periodical of their choice for their first two years in the department. The message behind the gift of these resources is a simple one. There is much to be learned about teaching, but not all of it is knowledge that needs to be acquired in the school of hard knocks.

I'd look carefully at the first-year teaching assignment in terms of what the new person is qualified to teach and whether he or she has experience doing so. New course preps are a part of new teaching assignments but in reasonable amounts—not three a semester or term, or five during the first year. Confidence comes with repetition. Let the new person teach the course two semesters in a row even if somebody else usually teaches it during the spring or if it's not typically offered again until the next year. I'd also look at class size. The less teaching experience, the greater the trauma associated with a big class. That's not an empirical conclusion but large courses require sophisticated pedagogical skills and typically should not be part of a first-year teaching experience.

I'd try to develop a climate of collegiality within the department, particularly with respect to teaching. We know that most of the ideas faculty acquire about teaching come from colleagues. I'd work to cultivate that exchange and make sure that new faculty are part of the dialogue. I'd put instructional topics on department meeting agendas—what are we doing together and separately to promote academic integrity? How do we develop critical thinking skills? Who's using group work and with what success? I might try to establish a mentoring program or sponsor a series of noontime discussions on instructional issues.

New faculty (in fact all faculty) need information about students. Student populations are changing dramatically. They are more diverse. They are older and must work more to pay for college. They are less well prepared (at least as measured by conventional faculty standards). They have learning styles markedly different than faculty. And you cannot teach them well unless you know who they are and how they learn.

I wouldn't be uptight about summative end-of-course evaluations for new faculty either. In fact, if I had my druthers, I'd absolve all new faculty from having to do them during their first year. I'd prescribe in their place a whole series of diagnostic, descriptive, formative activities (like midcourse evaluations, classroom research techniques, reciprocal observations with a colleague, videotaping small group instructional diagnosis, to name a few) that give the teacher the kind of specific, detailed feedback necessary to understand the impact of one's teaching behaviors, policies, and practices on student learning. If I was worried about a new faculty completing enough of the activities, I'd hook them up with the Teaching Excellence Center (if one exists on campus) or designate a senior faculty member as the resident resource on the topic. Why this radical approach? We know that teaching behaviors are most malleable to change during the first years of teaching. That propensity to innovate, try alternatives, and experiment is encouraged when it happens in an environment where it is safe to fail, at least occasionally.

Finally, I'd work diligently to fairly represent the hard work that is inherently a part of good teaching. Teaching still isn't rewarded as it ought to be (but that's another letter), but even those of us committed to instructional excellence often devalue teaching by the way we think and talk about it. Good teaching cannot be assumed or taken as given. In most new faculty, it must be consciously and systematically developed. We also devalue teaching by talking only in terms of technique. Getting students to participate in class is much more than a repertoire of techniques. Real teaching skill resides in the management and use of the repertoire. Getting students to do the reading is more than the "right" quiz strategy. Creating a classroom climate that is inclusive demands much more than instructor decree. To value teaching means to acknowledge its complexity and inherent intellectual intrigue. New faculty will acquire respect for teaching if they see their department head demonstrating that respect.

Dr. Weimer's comments illustrate the importance of mentoring for good teaching. Most teachers are not born; they need to be developed, and the first year is crucial for this development. Department chairs are instrumental for creating a climate that supports teaching by providing direct support for the new teacher. Again, we do not mean to suggest that the department chair must do this alone and be all things to all new faculty. Instead, we advocate the department chair taking a leadership role by modeling good mentoring and encouraging good teaching through very specific acts like those mentioned by Professor Weimer.

RESEARCH-FOCUSED SUPPORT

We now turn to a discussion of research and how it can be supported throughout the first year. As with all aspects of faculty development and socialization, many chairs assume that new faculty members are doing fine with their scholarly work if they do not hear otherwise. Unfortunately, this approach can lead to disaster for the new faculty member. Suddenly, a conference paper is due amidst everything else that needs to be done, and the overwhelmed professor ends up handing in a rough draft at best or deciding to table the conference until the following year. Without some support and mentoring, new faculty may find themselves responding to the immediate pressures of teaching and committee work and neglecting their own research. Chairs can be supportive of research through workshops (discussed later in this chapter) and by making it possible for new faculty members to have research assistants to aid in their teaching and research work.

Perhaps the most challenging aspect to the research component of faculty work is its diversity. Research involves the actual doing of research (i.e., collecting data), writing for presentation or publication, making presentations, finding grants, writing grants, and a lot of editing as writing cuts across all these domains. Depending on institutional standards for promotion and tenure, new faculty may find themselves involved in more or less of these research activities. Jim Fairweather's research, published in *Faculty Work and the Public Trust,* suggests that research is becoming a higher priority at campuses regardless of institutional type. This is not to say that every faculty member must be a prolific scholar; however, it does say that research is a higher stakes activity than teaching and service. The chair can communicate the institution's stance on research and can provide mechanisms to support new faculty as they begin to research for tenure and promotion.

We focus our suggestions for research on writing as it cuts across so many aspects of doing research. These suggestions come, in part, from Boice's research (1992) on new faculty as writers. The best writing practices and schedules need to come from the faculty members themselves. However, not all faculty members are natural writers and therefore may need some help and direction in establishing priorities in this area. For many, research is a private act (and often that translates to fretting alone about all that needs to be done). The following list provides some ideas for getting the new faculty member started (or recharged) to write for research and publication. These activities can be incorporated into departmental orientations that last throughout the first year. Encourage new faculty to do the following:

- **Write regularly throughout the semester/quarter.** Waiting for weekends, breaks, or summer is a form of procrastination. Productive writers are those that write regularly and do not let long periods of time lapse amidst a project. Writing an hour a day keeps the project alive and helps researchers make continual progress.

- **Share their work with colleagues both on and off campus.** Getting papers published and grants funded is hard work. It requires a lot of revision and resilience. By sharing written work with colleagues before it goes out, faculty not only increase the likelihood of acceptance but also remain constantly involved in the profession. Sharing work with fellow faculty, both on campus and off, ideally situates the new faculty member to establish professional networks and to become known in the field, both of which are helpful when the promotion and tenure review comes around in that the likelihood that external reviewers will be familiar with the person's work is increased.

- **Talk to you, as chair, about their writing projects.** Dropping by the new faculty member's office to ask how it is going and what projects they are working on can be a big help to the stalled writer. Writing tends to be private, and therefore, it is difficult to determine how professors are doing and whether they feel they are being productive. Simply talking about writing with the new faculty member is a way to indicate its importance and to encourage productivity.

On campuses where grant-funded research is a priority, the department chair needs to help faculty identify sources of funding, point faculty in the direction of campus personnel who support sponsored research activities, and connect new faculty with existing projects. These suggestions can help faculty get into the research network. Faculty with limited experience in obtaining grants cannot be expected to become sudden experts just because it is viewed by the administration as a favorable activity. Direct mentoring and orientation throughout the year can encompass these types of activities through things like department sponsored grant-writing workshops, a meeting with the research administration office, and presentations by faculty who have been successful in grant writing and administration.

We close this discussion on research with a letter from Robert Boice, author of *First-Order Principles for College Teachers: Ten Basic Ways to Improve the Teaching Process* and *The New Faculty Member*, a must-read book for department chairs and all faculty. We asked Boice, "If a department chair asked you for advice on how to work with junior faculty to develop productive researchers, what would you tell them?"

HELPING NEWCOMERS BECOME PRODUCTIVE RESEARCHERS
Advice from Robert Boice

When department chairs ask me for ideas about helping new faculty as productive scholars, I encourage them to consider two things: 1) where novice writers in academic careers typically derail, and 2) what exemplary chairs do that proves most helpful to writers. Both discussions bring up things that often get overlooked.

I begin by asking chairs to guess about the usual sequence of problems that lead to disappointing levels of productivity. Most chairs show the perspicacity that got them into leadership positions: They correctly imagine that new faculty who struggle as writers have too many bad beginnings, too little time, and too many distractions. They then tell me they are primed to hear what research says about predictable patterns of nonproductivity. Briefly, this is the common, modal sequence for writing problems in professorial careers:

First, warning signs occur in graduate school as displays of rushing and busyness that obscure delayed writing. Writing becomes fearsome, and it gets put off amid a frenzy of overcommitments to other things. The second crucial experience follows from the first. Dissertations are put on the back burner, sometimes for years, while things like temporary jobs take precedence.

The third symptom of trouble shows up most clearly amongst newcomers to professorial careers. Writing becomes excessively private and perfectionistic; colleagues are not allowed to do some of the work, especially to see early plans and drafts. The fourth predictable step is also about excessiveness. Unproductive writers are most likely to overinvest in preparations for teaching by preparing too much to say and presenting it too rapidly. Meanwhile, they have little time left for writing, exercising, socializing, or surviving.

The fifth step in this sad scenario comes by the second or third year, when colleagues and administrators begin providing feedback on progress toward retention and tenure. Because nonproductive writers find ways to deny their problems, they react with surprise and distress when told that they are failing as writers—the domain that academics, including themselves, value and reward most—and they react with anger when they notice that the other things they have been working so hard at (usually teaching and service) earn little or no commendation. This experience makes writing seem more pressuring, more aversive, and more detrimental to teaching. And even if these newcomers do write enough to manage tenure, the die has been cast: Writing hereafter will be sporadic and painful. (So it is that the vast majority of the professoriate do not publish.)

In my experience, immediate responses to this scenario are dominated by disbelief and discomfort. It all sounds so pervasive and irreversible that many chairs feel like giving up attempts to help: "Well look, what can I do? It starts before they even get here." Something else invariably comes up: "Oh (sighs), who am I to tell someone else how to get writing done? I'm not exactly prolific myself."

This is where I like to move to the second consideration. It shows what chairs do that actually helps new faculty manage more productivity. (And it reveals that none of the crucial acts demand special expertise or success as a writer.) Most importantly, it suggests that chairs play a far greater role in the success of their new hires than is generally appreciated.

Analysis of quick starters, new faculty who readily thrive as scholarly writers and as teachers, shows that they are disproportionately associated with chairs who display impressive commonalities. That is, exemplary novices tend to have exemplary chairpeople. These chairs, for example, hire with an "eyes-open" approach, mindfully attending to patterns that are widely known to predict productivity in professorial careers (e.g., timely completion of dissertations, publications in graduate school, moderate levels of busyness and commitments). They help arrange connections with models, mentors, collaborators, and friends before new hires arrive on campus (more so for women and minorities). Exemplary chairs begin early at helping new hires build portfolios of what they have published, what they are doing, and what they are planning as scholars, researchers, grant-getters, and writers. They draw new faculty into conversations (even weekly group discussions) about writing in ways that make it less private and more supported. And, most surprising, these exemplary chairs find ways to help new faculty make teaching and writing more interrelated and more mutually beneficial (e.g., by recognizing the counterproductive reluctance of new faculty to talk about their scholarship in their classrooms).

When I present this information, chairs usually remain silent for a moment or two. Then they return to some old reservations and questions: "Doesn't this mean that exemplary chairs spend so much time with new faculty that other chairing responsibilities get neglected?" (No.) "Don't exemplary chairs have to be exemplary producers to help in these ways?" (No.) "Won't new hires see all this as an intrusion?" (No, no, a thousand times no.) And, "isn't there something immoral about helping people master skills they should be able to manage on their own (after all, I did)?" (No, not unless you can overlook what happens to nontraditional newcomers to the professoriate who are typically denied access to old-boy networks and tacit knowledge about success.)

What comes, in the long run, of my advice? For chairs who keep talking about it, who try it, there are consistent reports of happy experiences in helping new faculty find more productivity. How can readers of this mere letter find similar benefits? Perhaps by finding a similar conversation of their own. Exemplary chairs, I often note, talk about and read about chairing. They take risks and try new things. They even report benefiting more than their new faculty from practicing all this.

Cordially,

Bob Boice
former Professor of Psychology
State University of New York at Stony Brook

THE FIRST YEAR

A productive first year is crucial to the ultimate success of any faculty member. Mentoring and orientation activities need to center around unit standards. In some departments, these activities are formal and addressed in monthly meetings throughout the first year. In other departments, faculty are supported more informally, primarily through conversations between newcomers and their chair and other members of the department. Regardless of whether the preferred approach is formal or informal, the important part is that orientation and mentorship must be deliberate. Leaving the transition up to the faculty member is a sure way to guarantee failure. While most faculty do know how to do their jobs, they still need support and advice on how to do their jobs well and how to do them in a way that matches departmental and institutional expectations.

The first year is perhaps the most crucial for junior faculty success. A faculty member who receives a good start is more likely to continue in that vein. As increasing numbers of new faculty enter the profession, department chairs can benefit from formalizing opportunities for socialization into the department and the institution. Mentors play a key role in helping faculty become acclimated and socialized to their new environments. The involved department chair is sure to play a role in this mentoring relationship, but it can also be shared with other senior faculty. The important thing to remember is that the new faculty member needs at least one person to turn to in the event of questions that range from how to get a new printer to what journals are highly regarded for publication. Faculty need ongoing contact with a mentor throughout their first year.

Collegiality is likely to be another area of concern for the new faculty member. No one wants to work in an environment that is unwelcoming and inhibiting. Chairs can play their part in creating collegial environments by first assessing the environment to determine if it is hospitable to newcomers (with an eye toward how women and faculty of color experience the departmental culture). With this information, chairs can help establish opportunities to create positive and constructive working environments for new and existing faculty. This constructive environment may include monthly colloquia, guest speakers, and/or social gatherings that give all members of the department the opportunity to become involved in departmental affairs.

All the activities we have suggested in this section take into account that orientation is a long-term process. Clearly, the success of a department's orientation depends on whether participants find the first session helpful and will look forward to follow-up meetings. At the end of this section, we have provided an outline of a year-long orientation process and a list of topics to consider when planning orientation activities for new faculty throughout their first year.

New faculty orientation that lasts throughout the first year creates a meaningful way to impart information new faculty members will need as issues arise and as they adjust to a new system, new policies and procedures, and new colleagues. Topics to cover in this orientation should include areas of general concern in addition to productivity in the areas of teaching, research, and service. Creating an environment where new faculty can thrive not only benefits the new faculty member but also the department, students, and the institution. We now turn to issues related to ongoing faculty development in Part III, "Developing Faculty Beyond the First Year."

CHECKLIST: TOPICS TO INCLUDE IN YEAR-LONG ORIENTATION PROGRAMS

General

☐ Managing time effectively

☐ Learning who is whom in the campus structure

☐ Managing stress

☐ Understanding promotion and tenure

☐ Finding a mentor

Teaching

☐ Developing a syllabus

☐ Selecting textbooks for class

☐ Conducting midcourse evaluations of teaching

☐ Interpreting teaching evaluations

☐ Using technology in the classroom

☐ Inviting teaching observations (formal and informal)

☐ Providing an overview of teaching tools available on campus

Research

☐ Establishing collaboration

☐ Tips for publishing

☐ Applying for internal grants

☐ Applying for external grants

☐ Peer review of writing

☐ Overview of publications in the field

Service

☐ Overview of requirements for service

☐ Types of service

☐ Description of relative importance of committees

☐ Disciplinary versus institutional service

- ☐ Professional outreach
- ☐ Consulting
- ☐ Extension activities

CHECKLIST: SAMPLE FORMAT FOR YEAR-LONG DEPARTMENTAL ORIENTATION

What we provide here is an example of what a comprehensive orientation for new faculty might include. The content and format of the sessions will vary depending on what is available in terms of orientation at the campus level and what the institutional priorities are for faculty success. These sessions can involve both new and returning faculty and are a good way to call upon the human resources in the department and develop camaraderie.

Session 1: Getting Started
If there is no whole-campus orientation, provide information (or where to find information) about:

- ☐ Benefits and insurance
- ☐ "Who's who" (e.g., president, vice presidents, provost, deans)
- ☐ Campus resources (e.g., research office, teaching center)
- ☐ Faculty union if the faculty is governed by a collective bargaining agreement

At the departmental level, introductory information should include:

- ☐ Introductions of all faculty in the department including their areas of teaching, research, and service
- ☐ Overview of departmental policies and procedures
- ☐ Departmental priorities for the year
- ☐ Departmental and institutional standards for promotion and tenure

Session 2: Planning to Succeed
- ☐ Overview of department's academic standards
- ☐ Discussion of how these standards fit with institution-wide standards

☐ Presentation on the goals of the institution and how new faculty fit into those goals

☐ Demonstration of good practices for keeping documentation of accomplishments up to date and well organized

Session 3: Becoming an Effective Teacher

☐ Strategies for planning a course

☐ Alternatives to the lecture

☐ Presentation by the instructional developer (if available) or by faculty who have won teaching awards

☐ Presentation by technology experts to talk about technology in the classroom

☐ Overview of evaluation options to assess teaching effectiveness (e.g., midsemester evaluations)

☐ Discussion of how teaching fits into department and university standards for promotion

Session 4: Developing a Research Agenda

☐ Explanation of institutional priorities for research

☐ Overview of what constitutes research

☐ How to develop a plan of research for the tenure track years

☐ Presentation by faculty who have been successful in getting external grants and/or a person from the research office (if relevant for your campus)

☐ Discussion of publications—how and where to get published

☐ Discussion of the most common pitfalls to research productivity

Session 5: Getting Involved in Service

☐ Overview of committees at the campus, college, and department levels

☐ Discussion of expectations for involvement in committees

☐ Getting involved in disciplinary associations—how and which ones

☐ Expectations for public service

Session 6: Planning for the Future

☐ Overview of what's involved in annual reviews, promotion reviews, and tenure reviews, and schedule of formal reviews

☐ What it takes to be an associate professor, a full professor

☐ Presentation by people at different stages of the process

REFERENCES

Boice, R. (1992). *The new faculty member: Supporting and fostering professional development.* San Francisco, CA: Jossey-Bass.

Boice, R. (1996). *First-order principles for college teachers: Ten basic ways to improve the teaching process.* Bolton, MA: Anker.

Eble, K. E. (1990). *The craft of teaching: A guide to mastering the professor's art* (2nd ed.). San Francisco, CA: Jossey-Bass.

Fairweather, J. S. (1996). *Faculty work and the public trust.* Boston, MA: Allyn & Bacon.

Hutchings, P. (1996). *Making teaching community property: A menu for peer collaboration and peer review.* Washington, DC: AAHE.

McKeachie, W. J. (1994). *Teaching tips: Strategies, research, and theory for college and university teachers* (9th ed.). Lexington, MA: D. C. Heath and Company.

Nilson, L. B. (1998). *Teaching at its best: A research-based resource for college instructors.* Bolton, MA: Anker.

Weimer, M. (1990). *Improving college teaching: Strategies for developing instructional effectiveness.* San Francisco, CA: Jossey-Bass.

Weimer, M. (1996). *Improving your classroom teaching.* Newbury Park, CA: Sage.

PART III

DEVELOPING FACULTY BEYOND THE FIRST YEAR

I was really naive about tenure; I had no exposure to it or discussions about it. So, I really was in the dark and I started out just trying to figure out what it was all about.

To be quite honest, after two and a half years I still am not completely sure. There are no written numbers; you start to figure it out from the rumor mill, from persons who have gone through the tenure process in the past.

I wish someone would tell me exactly what I need to do. What we get told when we come here is that we need to publish in the highest quality journals. We are told that the research has to contribute to our discipline and that it needs to be recognized by other researchers. There are no informal guidelines of how much of what kind of work constitutes enough to get tenure. If you have one article, one single article that everybody cites, is that enough? (Tierney & Bensimon, 1996, p. 109).

———

People in our department get along pretty well. Our graduate program is just starting to take off, and it's been good for us to have a common goal. Even though I'm new in the department I feel really comfortable. As a student and then as a visiting instructor at the university where I went to graduate school, I felt so integrated so I really was nervous about starting a new position. The transition has been smooth. Now that I'm in my second year it really seems like my first year was all-in-all pretty good. The chair here really looks out for her faculty. She sends us to workshops, provides refreshments for a research colloquium once a semester, and observes everyone's classes at least once a year. She's very good at making our department a fun and stimulating place to work. She makes people feel included. Everyone seems genuinely interested in one another's work. I'd say we are a pretty collegial department.

Thus far, we have dedicated our discussion to issues surrounding the hiring and first-year orientation of new faculty. In this final part of the book, the focus is on the development and socialization of new faculty beyond the first year. We include mentoring in this section because, although it begins in the first year, mentoring is a vital aspect of developing new faculty while they work toward tenure in their first several years as an assistant professor.

Isolation and loneliness often characterize the first year of a new faculty position. This is not surprising given the magnitude of change a new position can involve. For most, a new position means a new town, a substantial relocation, a new set of colleagues, expanding expectations, and new institutional and departmental cultures to negotiate. Departmental colleagues play a crucial role in helping new faculty make a smooth transition into their positions.

Junior faculty socialization must be deliberate—department chairs cannot just rely on people getting along or, as discussed in the previous section, on the new faculty member knowing what questions to ask. Departmental culture and climate can vary considerably, and not everyone experiences the culture in the same way. While one faculty member may find the departmental culture to be very open and welcoming, another may find it alienating. Does this mean that something is wrong with the person having difficulties finding their way? No, what it means is that people have different reactions to organizational settings. Deliberate, ongoing mentoring in the first year can help assure that all faculty have a positive experience as they enter into a new departmental culture.

What do we mean by culture? Two important aspects of culture warrant mention here: 1) Culture is produced from the social relations of the participants within an organization, and 2) culture changes as new individuals and groups enter into it. Rather than trying to convince the new faculty member having difficulty fitting in that her perceptions are mistaken, the chair of the department needs to be intentional about trying to determine how the social relations that characterize the department might be experienced from the standpoint of the newcomer. The possibility exists that what is viewed as friendly and informal by old-timers may feel like insiderism and poor communication to a newcomer who remains outside the social circle. Not unlike an ethnographer, chairs can decipher the culture of their departments in order to anticipate potential barriers to the successful integration of new professors.

As we have stressed in the first two sections, a good start is invaluable for new faculty as they take on their new roles. Equally important, however, is the ongoing socialization of junior faculty beyond the first year, particularly in the area of the promotion and tenure process. As illustrated in the excerpted comments above, confusion may exist beyond the first few weeks, months, or year, if communication breaks down. Department chairs are a vital link for faculty to establish themselves as effective teachers, researchers, and contributing members of the department, campus, and discipline.

Study after study about life on the tenure track points out that an implicit assumption exists among chairs and senior faculty that junior faculty, once hired, know what they have to do in order to succeed. In research universities, an expectation exists that the newcomer will know the importance of publishing and will make that a priority; smaller teaching-oriented institutions expect faculty to excel in teaching and to dedicate time to students by being available to meet with them on a regular basis. Despite institutional differences in the expectations for new faculty, most institutions and academic departments do not have an existing structure to guide new faculty toward successful promotion and tenure.

All institutions provide entering faculty with a copy of the institution's promotion and tenure guidelines and faculty handbooks, but as we all know, the objective of such publications is not to instruct the newcomer on what to do but rather to explicate the formal aspects of the process. Like mission statements, promotion and tenure guidelines seem to be purposefully ambiguous in order to accommodate interdisciplinary and departmental differences. While we are by no means advocating that institutions tell junior faculty the number of articles they should publish or that they should have a specified number of articles published in journals A, B, and C, academic chairs should recognize (as exemplified by the quotes above) that the anxiety junior faculty seem to live with in the first six years of their academic career can be alleviated.

In this part, we discuss the chair's role in helping new faculty negotiate the specifics of promotion and tenure. Chapter 10 addresses the role mentoring plays in faculty integration and explores one-to-one mentoring relationships in addition to more communal perspectives on mentoring by examining ways in which department chairs can foster departmental collegiality. Chapter 11 examines how assistant professors are evaluated for promotion and tenure and offers specifics of the process. In this chapter we also discuss stress and time management. In Chapter 12, we address the chair's role in developing effective researchers and in Chapter 13, developing effective teachers. The focus of Chapter 14 is the chair's role in monitoring service obligations. We conclude this part with Chapter 15, an overall discussion of the procedural aspects of the evaluation process.

REFERENCE

Tierney, W. G., & Bensimon, E. M. (1996). *Promotion and tenure: Community and socialization in academe.* Albany, NY: SUNY Press.

·⇒ CHAPTER 10 ⇐·

CREATING MENTORING RELATIONSHIPS AND FOSTERING COLLEGIALITY

The department chair came in and talked with me yesterday, as a matter of fact, and sat right where you are now. He suggests places to publish my work, reads everything I write, and gives feedback. We talk all the time. He meets with all of us. He gives me things that he thinks are helpful. He met with me after the second- and fourth-year review and made sure I understood what was meant. That was good because those letters can be confusing. They write something and you can blow it out of proportion or you might miss something. He's very easy to talk to, and he also protects the junior faculty from the fights that happen from time to time in the department.

I chose a mentor, and it's been a very positive relationship. It's very important as far as I am concerned, in terms of understanding this particular system and setting my priorities so that by the time the tenure clock rolls around, I will be ready.

Some new faculty may view mentoring as an idealistic relationship between an established member of the profession, who is willing to use his or her status in the field and institution on behalf of the newcomer, and a new faculty member. The combination of this romanticized vision and the ambiguity of what constitutes mentoring can lead to disappointment for the new faculty member. Not all faculty members can be as lucky as the

113

one above who has a strong mentor in her department chair. It is fairly common for junior faculty to complain that no mentors are available or that their assigned mentor does not have the time to meet with them; some faculty also view the relationship as too artificial. Although the desirability of establishing mentors for newcomers is widely shared, few departments actually have structured ways of creating mentoring relationships or of determining whether they work. Mentoring tends to happen accidentally, and as a consequence, not all newcomers who stand to benefit from such relationships are able to establish them.

ESTABLISHING MENTORING RELATIONSHIPS

The department chair's role in facilitating mentoring relationships for new faculty varies considerably. In some departments, like the one mentioned at the outset of this chapter, the chair is a mentor to all faculty and plays an active role in their development. In other departments, chairs assign each new person an experienced faculty member to act as a mentor for the transition. Other units have structured programs, such as a college-wide mentor matching program, whereby each new person is assigned a mentor to help negotiate tenure requirements, give advice on teaching, identify appropriate service positions, and understand advising functions. Unfortunately, most departments just leave it up to the individual to ask for help if he needs it and to seek out his own mentors.

Ideally, mentoring relationships will just grow organically, but in most instances this is not the case. If department chairs are serious about developing new faculty, mentoring must be deliberate. This is not to say that every department or college needs to have a structured and formal mentor program; however, it does mean that department chairs can take an active role in mentoring new faculty and in facilitating connections with all faculty so mentoring relationships can develop. Each new faculty member needs a designated mentor or mentor committee to help with the transition of a new position.

New faculty often feel afloat in a sea of work and confusion in their first year. Many in academe operate under the false assumption that if a new hire has made it to the faculty ranks, then that person knows what to do as faculty member. An assigned mentor can help new faculty prioritize and set goals for their work beyond the classroom. Ideally, a mentor can answer questions a new faculty member may not want to ask a chair or other authority figure.

The most important criterion in selection of a mentor is effectiveness in either one or a combination of the following areas: teaching, research, and institutional citizenship. Certainly, one person cannot be all things to the new faculty member (thus, the notion of a mentoring team); however, mentors can pass on advice and skills in areas in which they have familiarity and success. Because mentors play an integral role in helping new faculty make the transition to a new position, the purpose of mentoring at the outset is to ensure that the new faculty member begins and continues to head in the right direction. All mentors should be familiar with promotion and tenure procedures and policies and be willing to be involved in a mentoring relationship.

Good Mentor Pairs

When identifying suitable mentor pairs, the following list provides areas to consider:

- Compatibility in career goals

- Commonalities in personal circumstances or interests (e.g., family status, sports activities)

- Productivity in common areas (i.e., if the new faculty member is expected to publish, match that person with a faculty member who has a successful publication record)

- New pairings (it is best not to match people with previous relationships)

The key to matching mentoring pairs is commitment to time. Some pairings will result in little more than informal meetings whereby the mentor acts as a sounding board, while other pairs may develop career-long collaborations. The chair's role is to create mentoring relationships and monitor their success.

Good mentors are...
- familiar with the department, college, and campus

- positive about their positions

- productive as teachers, scholars, and/or institutional citizens

- willing to spend time with a newcomer on an individual basis

- politically aware

- understanding of the challenges presented by new faculty

- willing to reach out to new faculty members

- supportive of new faculty in the department

- good listeners

In their book *Chairing an Academic Department,* Gmelch and Miskin (1995) directly address the issue of faculty support through mentoring and offer several guidelines for mentoring that we call upon here. Gmelch and Miskin illustrate the important roles department chairs play in both direct mentoring of new faculty and in creating a climate where faculty will mentor one another.

THE ANNUAL PLAN

Faculty positions tend to be fairly autonomous, and most prefer it that way. Mentoring does not discount autonomy; instead, at its very core, mentoring shows genuine concern for faculty progress and development. Faculty work at most institutions centers around teaching, research, and service. Faculty support should encompass what Gmelch and Miskin refer to as an annual plan that keeps new hires moving toward their goals. This plan keeps both the faculty member and the department chair apprised of the new member's progress. The annual plan is a way to overcome the ambiguity of what new faculty should do to accomplish personal, professional, and departmental goals in the first year and beyond. It is also a proactive way to nurture good habits and encourage planning in a manner that is not intrusive or meddling.

The plan should be personalized to meet the needs of both the department and the new faculty member and include areas such as writing (e.g., short- and long-term goals), teaching (e.g., plans for new courses), and service (e.g., projections for levels of involvement) with the new faculty member developing his/her own plan. Mentors (or department chairs) can help junior faculty define a plan and see their goals through to completion. The annual plan can also be helpful for department chairs to debrief with faculty at their annual reviews. The following is a sample annual plan for Deborah, a new sociology faculty member in a doctoral-granting institution where expectations center equally around teaching and research with anticipated service involvement. This type of plan will help her stay focused throughout the year.

SAMPLE ANNUAL PLAN FOR THE FIRST YEAR

Research Goals

- Establish a research agenda with a focused line of inquiry.

- Make connections to fellow faculty with similar interests to develop the potential for collaboration.

- Submit one conference proposal.

- Submit one article for publication.

Writing

1. Work on dissertation to prepare for publication.

2. Send drafts of article to three colleagues for feedback (1 local, 1 dissertation advisor, 1 national).

3. Attend faculty development workshops on writing and research.

4. Brainstorm for conference proposal.

Publication

1. Incorporate comments from colleagues and submit article for publication.

2. Submit conference proposal.

3. Meet with department chair to discuss short- and long-term research and publication goals and solicit suggestions on how to best meet these goals.

Grants

1. Collect information about internal grant opportunities campus-wide.

2. Submit "minigrant" application for new faculty summer research projects.

Teaching Goals

- Prepare for spring courses.

- Limit class preparation and grading to no more than teaching days (Monday, Wednesday, Friday—fall semester; Tuesday and Thursday—spring semester).

- Say no to summer teaching for the first year.

    1. Prepare syllabi for spring.

    2. Submit book requests.

    3. Have at least one person come to class to do an informal evaluation of spring and fall courses.

    4. Conduct midterm evaluation of fall courses and incorporate information into courses for fall and spring.

Service Goals

- Collect information about departmental, college, and university priorities.

- Find out about committees that will help acclimate the newcomer to campus.

    1. Say no to committee work for the first year (at a minimum the first semester).

    2. Meet with department chair to strategize service commitments for the first year.

While this sample plan is for a first-year faculty member, annual plans should continue throughout the junior faculty member's career. Annual reviews and goal-setting sessions with the chair or mentor can help junior faculty understand the institution's expectations, and can aid them in meeting those expectations.

Mentoring for research development may fall to the chair or to a senior member in the department whose research most closely coincides with the new faculty member's work. Regular meetings between the mentor and new faculty member to discuss progress and a written plan for research can be essential in providing the direction a new faculty member needs. A research plan should not wait until the end of the first year, but should begin right away. A plan for meetings to discuss teaching, research, and service (i.e., the annual plan) might look like this:

- Meet with new faculty member to go over the faculty handbook or orientation information and answer questions or address concerns about promotion and tenure within the first two weeks of employment.

- Midway through the first semester (or about three months into the appointment), meet with new faculty to find out if they have questions or need additional information about the tenure process or any information they have received. This meeting should address specific questions about research and should also focus on how well the faculty member is maintaining a balance between teaching, research, and service (remember, successful faculty in the realm of research are those that incorporate research into their workload from the start).

- At the above meeting, have the faculty member develop a list of goals for writing and research. This can include a portfolio of items that are currently in progress (e.g., developing the dissertation into a publication) or plans for the future. This portfolio can become the basis of discussion for future meetings.

- During the second semester (or between six and nine months into the appointment) touch base to see how things are progressing with research and teaching.

- At the end of one year, conduct the first annual review and develop teaching and research goals for the summer and year two.

- At the outset of year two, meet with junior faculty to assess the summer's progress and to go over research plans for the coming year. This may include going over plans for conferences and discussing ways to accomplish research goals. Chairs can be particularly helpful in maintaining contact so that things like conference papers become articles for publication.

- At the end of each subsequent year, meet to review progress toward goals and to establish new goals and work plans for the following year. This review will be especially important around the third year review for tenure and promotion.

This kind of plan helps the chair or mentor maintain regular contact with junior faculty, to continue development of the portfolio, and to monitor progress with meeting research goals. Reviews, whether they are annual or every three years, should not be a time for faculty to be surprised by their progress. Maintaining regular progress reviews will help to avoid such a reaction from the junior faculty member.

THE MENTORING RELATIONSHIP

Most faculties are composed of considerable talent. Part of the department chair's role as mentor is to let new and existing faculty know of one another's accomplishments and interests so as to create fertile ground for collegiality. These types of activities can take the shape of a research symposium or colloquium, or informal gatherings such as brown bag lunches. This type of promotion also allows students to learn of faculty interests. This is especially important to the new faculty member who does not have an established reputation. Taking a proactive stance to celebrate faculty accomplishments is not only good practice for individual faculty, but for the department as a whole.

Perhaps the chair's most important role is to lead and mentor by example. Maintaining an active service, research, and teaching agenda, and making faculty aware of your schedule, is perhaps the best way to mentor the new faculty member.

These activities suggested by Gmelch and Miskin illustrate that mentoring is more than a one-to-one relationship between mentor and protégé. These suggestions are ways to provide individual mentoring and, perhaps more importantly, bring faculty together as colleagues who can support and mentor one another. The scenario that follows illustrates one type of mentor relationship.

Scenario: Millie is a new faculty member at a large research university that has an established mentoring program for all incoming faculty. The program matches new faculty members with seasoned faculty within their college or school. Millie's experience with the program has been fairly successful in terms of learning the ropes and having a helping hand to guide her through the first year. Millie's mentor has provided valuable information on departmental politics, unit standards, and who is whom on campus. Millie is afraid, however, that her assigned mentor is not very good at giving advice on research and publication. In fact, Millie feels like she is getting bad advice from her mentor about where to publish and the types of avenues to pursue.

Response: Chairs can provide support for newcomers by recognizing that no one person can fulfill all mentoring needs. Faculty development, like the faculty career itself, is multifaceted and requires support that runs the gamut of faculty expectations. Millie's experience illustrates the benefits of an established mentor program—it helped her get started in the first year and provided her with someone to talk to about departmental and institutional issues. However, her experience also illustrates the limitations of one mentor. Millie's mentor is of an older generation of faculty with different socialization experiences and different ideas about research. The solution to Millie's dilemma is to provide her with support and help her find an additional mentor that is compatible with her research directions.

Millie's experience makes clear that mentoring is not an isolated relationship solely focused on tenure rules, politics, and evaluation. Mentorship is a dynamic working relationship between two people who share common interests, with the mentor also acting as a guide. One-to-one mentoring relationships are important for new faculty; however, we support the notion of not just one mentor, but the possibility of many mentors, a situation that is likely to occur in departments with healthy collegiality.

FOSTERING COLLEGIALITY

I've spent a lot of time trying to figure out how to proceed with my scholarship. You know, where should I go now? I've done this dissertation; what's my next step as a scholar and as a teacher? I have so many little projects out there, and people are going to want to hear where these projects are going, and I realize that I need direction. . . . I need someone to help me figure that out. (Tierney & Bensimon, 1996, p. 117)

_____

I don't know how to ask people for help, and they don't know or don't care to give it.

_____

I'm the type of person who just will go out and have lunch and go drinking with anybody who'll tell me what's going on. But somebody who doesn't have that personality or isn't politically aware may be surprised. (Tierney & Bensimon, 1996, p. 110)

The term collegiality is used a great deal in colleges and universities. It conveys an idyllic image of the workplace, men and women working together with their students in the pursuit of knowledge. The reality, however, is that collegiality within an academic department, school, college, or university is rare. As the above excerpts illustrate, collegiality, or its lack, may have a great impact on all aspects of a new faculty member's career. In fact, lack of collegiality is a major stress factor for new faculty. Characteristics of the academic profession, such as hyper-specialization, autonomy, and the greater value placed on the norms of the discipline than on the local institutional culture, severely limit opportunities for sustained engagement among academics.

At present, higher education suffers deeply from the loss of community. Studies of faculty portray the academy as alienating, collegiality as hollowed, and faculty members as estranged from their immediate environment and colleagues. Professors report that they rarely engage in conversations about ideas or teaching. They feel uncertain about their performance, but have no one with whom to discuss problems. Moreover, they are reluctant to admit a lack of expertise. The individualistic model of faculty life means that new faculty are left to fend for themselves; the cultures of the academy in general and the department in particular too frequently do not engender a caring ethic. For newcomers, the absence of caring can be very demoralizing.

Obstacles to collegiality are the generational and value differences between junior and senior faculty, manifested in cultural conflicts. New PhD's have been socialized in their graduate programs to be researchers, in contrast to many senior faculty who were hired at a time when teaching was the primary activity. In many cases the chair will belong to the "older generation," and it is important that he/she understands how generational differences can hamper collegiality. Cultural and gender differences can also compound difficulties with creating a collegial environment. Any form of difference—whether it be based on age, culture, gender, sexual orientation, or ideology—can challenge departmental harmony. By becoming aware of the differences in their ranks, department chairs can work to include all colleagues into the department, so that deleterious cliques do not form.

We asked Professor Anna Neumann, a scholar of higher education who has been engaged in a longitudinal study of "colleagueship" (1993), if she would share with our readers her thoughts on what chairs might do to foster collegiality for newcomers. Her thoughtful response provides chairs with useful recommendations for enhancing departmental collegiality.

HELPING TO FOSTER COLLEGIALITY FOR NEWCOMERS
A Letter from Professor Anna Neumann

Collegiality is a much misunderstood word, and the expectations it raises, while admirable, can be unrealistic. Collegiality, in its conventional use, refers to the ideals of faculty life—professors collectively and harmoniously engaged in the pursuit of knowledge, the crafting of curriculum, and the planning of teaching programs. While the inhabitants of this idealized world don't always agree, they rely on reasoned discussion with peers and sage advice from "elders" to resolve the differences of opinion that emerge. Consensus rules in this collegial world.

I would argue that wishes for collegiality are, for the most part, just wishes, and that collegiality, while remaining an important ideal in academe is just that. In real life, professors are more likely to strive for collegiality than to achieve it. While collaboration exists, so does strife, an aspect of faculty life that the word "collegiality" does not pick up very well. To describe faculty relations as faculty members experience them—helpful, hurtful, and inconsequential—I prefer the word colleagueship because it brings forth both positive and negative aspects of faculty relations. Collegiality focuses mostly on the positive that we wish for.

But if we take the word colleagueship as our point of departure, what do we see? And what are the implications of what we see for department chairs working with pre-tenure faculty? Let me reiterate: Colleagueship, as I'm using it, refers to the range of relationships that may exist among professors—from friendship to contentiousness, from close and regular engagement to alienation, and everything in between. If you're a department chair who would like to enhance new faculty members' experiences of colleagueship, what might you do? Let me begin with some perspectives.

First, when junior faculty enter an institution and department for the first time, they are entering a web of well-established (though sometimes shifting) relationships, some positive, some negative, others neutral. These new faculty are, in essence, strangers—formally in the door of the department, yet outside the ebb and flow of its internal, colleague-based relationships. This colleagueship, whatever its quality, is, for the most part, not reflected in the university's bureaucratic structure, including its departments. For example, that a group of people belong to a particular department does not mean they agree, understand, support, or even know each other or each other's work. A new faculty member, especially one just out of graduate school, may be unaccustomed to—even unaware of—the ambiguity and discord of departmental life.

Second, a new faculty member is likely to be engaged in the crafting of her or his scholarly agenda, including the program of work that will inform her/his research and teaching for years to come. This person is probably learning in the best sense of the word. The relationships that she or he forms in the new department are likely to affect that learning, and importantly, what she or he becomes as a scholar and teacher. Thus while the new professor's scholarly values and interests are central to her/his work, the colleagueship that this person finds herself or himself in can be very formative. For these reasons, the colleague-based relationships that a new faculty member makes—or stumbles into—can be crucial. How might department chairs help? Here are some thoughts derived from my own writing on this subject.

1. Introductions and announcements that a new colleague has arrived are never enough. Help a new faculty member make substantive connections to campus-based colleagues who are working in areas related to the newcomer's expertise and/or interests. This is something you, as chair, should consider doing continuously for the newcomer during her/his early years on campus. For one thing, the new faculty member's interests may just be emerging, or it may take you a while to understand those interests in relation to the work that others on campus do. Inform established colleagues about the newcomer's interests in ways that will help them see the connections to their own work. Such links are not always immediately obvious.

2. Provide opportunities for junior faculty members to get to know each other as colleagues and friends. While competitiveness does sometimes grow among untenured peers, this need not be the case. The friendship that grows among junior faculty can grow into good colleagueship in the middle and senior years of their careers. Actively discourage competitiveness. One way to do this is to evaluate peers only in reference to their own accomplishments and not in comparison to each other. Another suggestion is to emphasize publicly the unique identities of junior faculty—for example, as reflected in their work—as opposed to speaking of them in ways that make them appear interchangeable. This is particularly important when the peers themselves are different from the majority of their senior colleagues—for example, two women or two ethnic minorities in a traditionally all-male department. While emphasizing the uniqueness of individuals, you might simultaneously applaud their efforts to work together in teaching, research, curriculum development, or other projects.

3. Introduce new faculty to departmental colleagues, but don't stop here. Help them get to know colleagues with related interests in other departments as well.

4. While junior faculty are often advised to avoid excessive committee commitments, some committee service that brings new professors into contact with other faculty (who might become future collaborators) can be a good thing. Help the new faculty member choose committee service that makes sense. But consider the other side of the coin as well: Discourage the newcomer's service on committees that are excessively politically entangled or that may draw the newcomer (unknowingly) into longstanding difficulties. However, alerting the newcomer about those difficulties is not a bad idea. Some department chairs may believe they are shielding newcomers by not talking to them about the politics of the new setting. Chances are that if a newcomer doesn't hear about departmental and institutional troubles (including feuds and alliances) from a senior colleague, she or he will learn about them the hard way—by falling into them.

5. Be aware that a new faculty member is stepping into a stream of institutional conversation—institutional meaning—that has been in progress for a long time. Be prepared to help the newcomer decipher words and deeds that make little or no sense to her or him. I wish you, and those to whom your handbook is addressed, my best as you—and they—continue in efforts to illuminate and humanize the experiences of new faculty.

Sincerely,

Anna Neumann
Associate Professor
Michigan State University

IMPEDIMENTS TO COLLEGIALITY

Collegiality can be impeded in a variety of ways. The newcomer's office might be segregated from most faculty offices, putting the individual at a disadvantage. However, physical proximity does not automatically lead to interaction. Many faculty complain that despite having adjacent offices or being just across the hall from colleagues, a lack of communication still exists; this lack of interaction is often symbolized by closed office doors.

The composition of the department can also make a difference, particularly if the newcomer stands out as different from the norm—the lone assistant professor in a department of long-tenured faculty, a woman assistant professor in a predominantly male department, or the only minority.

To a great extent, the problems of collegiality result from the attitudes and behaviors of senior faculty, many of whom are unaware of how their actions (or lack of actions) impact the perceptions of newcomers. Tenured faculty who have created their niches, adhere to their routines, and depend on established relationships can easily overlook the needs of newcomers. Some may feel that they made it on their own and the newcomers should as well. The most serious impediment to collegiality is the cultural conflict that develops between junior and senior faculty as a result of having been socialized at different times. Bob Boice (1992) and Elizabeth Whitt (1991) have both addressed the issue of how intergenerational differences can produce cultural conflict or the emergence of dual cultures within a department. This conflict may be manifested by 1) senior faculty excluding new faculty from decision-making about department affairs, either de facto or intentionally in the pretext of protecting them from internal politics, 2) senior faculty being resentful of newcomers' eagerness to gain recognition for their work and professional visibility, 3) senior faculty not showing interest or valuing the research of assistant professors, 4) senior faculty not extending invitations for lunch or other more social activities, and 5) senior faculty not making themselves accessible for more informal interactions. While many of these behaviors may be unintentional, others may be deliberate. As the head of the department, the chair can help to set the tone by actively working to create a more welcoming departmental culture.

STRATEGIES TO FOSTER COLLEGIALITY

What can chairs do to bridge the chasms that can exist between new and existing faculty? The following strategies call upon department chairs to take a leadership role in creating opportunities to build collegiality for newcomers.

- Schedule a lunch once a month with two assistant professors and two senior faculty to encourage informal discussion of departmental or institutional matters; use these opportunities to connect new faculty with one another and also with senior faculty.

- Schedule presentations of research in progress by faculty and students to stimulate exchange of ideas.

- Arrange for one or more senior professors to accompany newcomers to social gatherings such as a holiday party, an all-college faculty meeting, or some other form of event where a newcomer might feel like an outsider.

- Prior to the arrival of new faculty, hold a series of meetings with senior faculty to make them aware of how they can facilitate the newcomer's adaptation. Develop seminars or informal conversations to consider how the culture of the department may need to change with the entry of younger and possibly more diverse faculty.

- Involve junior faculty in decision-making and in conversations having to do with institutional or departmental matters. The chair's role, in part, is to educate new faculty as to how the institution and department work, including such things as the politics of the budget, curriculum, and faculty governance.

- Whenever appropriate, create opportunities for junior and senior faculty to collaborate (not as apprentice and master) in an area of shared interest such as developing a team-taught course or applying for a grant.

- Hold an annual retreat for junior faculty only to encourage bonding and discussion of common problems.

- Coach new faculty on how to be proactive about seeking mentors, feedback, and establishing connections.

Collegiality is a departmental ideal that, as we have pointed out, can be disrupted by generational and cultural differences. We now turn to a more specific discussion of how to cultivate collegiality in light of these differences. The department chair who takes care to create a collegial environment for women and racial and ethnic minorities will be creating a collegial setting for all.

WOMEN AND COLLEGIALITY

I have zero collegiality in my department. They don't know what I do. I feel alienated, not on an equal footing with the men. Sometimes I have lunch in the faculty club and see the

> *guys from my department eating together. In the three years I*
> *have been here, no one has asked me to have lunch. (Tierney*
> *& Bensimon, 1996, p. 89)*

Clearly this professor views the culture of her department as unfriendly. Her department chair, on the other hand, may be surprised to hear this. He has been in the department for a long time; several of the faculty members get together regularly for lunch; meetings are rarely held because there is so much informal conversation going on that they are not needed; and a very low level of conflict exists because consensus can be found about the curriculum, when courses should be taught, and who should teach them. However, this perspective shows that the chair has a narrow view of the department, neglecting to consider how a new female faculty member might react to the department's climate. Chairs need to be aware that the culture of the unit is experienced differently depending on perspective.

Being included as a colleague is a persistent concern for many women. Department chairs who may be supportive of hiring more women (and minorities) often are not cognizant that these one-of-a-kind faculty are frequently left to cope on their own with alienating department cultures. Studies of faculty report that women tend to take on more activities that put them in contact with others: They spend more time talking to and advising students, more time on teaching, and more time volunteering for service activities than do their male colleagues. Rather than viewing these activities as a woman's natural inclination, chairs should consider that they may be nothing more than opportunities for making contact and establishing connections with others. Department chairs who understand this phenomenon can be instrumental in providing women faculty with opportunities for establishing social and professional networks in order to eliminate time-consuming activities that may be detrimental to their careers and status (Tierney & Bensimon, 1996).

Collegiality is far more likely to occur when there is a shared orientation to the discipline. More women are now engaged in feminist scholarship, much of which challenges traditional concepts in the disciplines, and by extension, the legitimacy of the scholarship that senior faculty have been committed to as teachers and scholars. It is important that department chairs be sensitive to the increased vulnerability felt by women whose feminist or nontraditional work is criticized by senior faculty for being ideological or politically driven (Tierney & Bensimon, 1996). Similarly, women faculty who are just getting started with their academic careers may be familiar with new teaching approaches that are more student-centered and discussion-oriented, often running the risk of being criticized for eschewing lecturing and the traditional authority role. New female faculty members' transition into a predominately male department can be eased by a sensitive chair who provides access into the existing collegial structure.

COLLEGIALITY IN PREDOMINANTLY MALE DEPARTMENTS

> *There is a professor who jokes about white men not being able to get jobs... he says it jokingly, but you can tell he has serious feelings about it.... I think he accepts me now, but he was one of the senior faculty who did not want me here.... No one says anything to him... they shrug it off, they say "that is just the way he is."* (Tierney & Bensimon, 1996, p. 90).

In departments where faculty are predominantly male, women often feel they have to adhere to unspoken rules of collegiality and tolerate comments that may be made in jest but are nevertheless a form of backlash directed at women. To reduce the likelihood of situations like this one, chairs can be proactive in establishing departmental cultures that are women-affirming (Tierney & Bensimon, 1996). We offer two courses of action that will make male-dominated departments more welcoming to women.

1. Chairs can create opportunities to educate senior faculty to the behaviors and language that—while not overtly sexist—contributes to a chilly climate for their female colleagues. Chairs can also avail themselves of a variety of resources to plan these sessions, including the assistance of colleagues in Women's Studies or the women's center.

2. In situations like the one described above, chairs need to be aware that women assistant professors may find the comments made by colleagues offensive but not say anything for fear of retribution. The chair or other senior colleagues who witness such comments should be the ones to point out why they are offensive, rather than just shrugging it off as this woman's colleagues did. When those in power positions fail to intervene, they are encouraging a culture of disrespect for women.

As the most male-dominated disciplines, the sciences, engineering, and mathematics tend to present the greatest problems for the integration of women, and it is fairly common to hear female professors in these fields complain about loneliness and feelings of competence.

> *In the math department, it's a very lonely experience. Math is a very male subject... the expectation of how a mathematician thinks, or how a mathematician operates are very masculine expectations. A lot of mathematicians tend to be very aggressive people, very argumentative... and that is not my personality at all... part of it is just me, but I think in general, female mathematicians tend to be not nearly so argumentative as the males... so I find it very difficult to operate in that sort of environment; it is very hard to handle.* (Tierney & Bensimon, 1996, p. 90).

Women-Affirming Chairs

> *In this department, being a woman is great. We have a lot of them. Of the five junior faculty, three are women. My colleagues treat me as though they think I am smart and that I am worthy of consideration when we are debating.* (Tierney & Bensimon, 1996, p. 94).

> *They have done a very nice job of recruiting women, and so I would say for the most part there aren't a lot of gender issues. I have not ever been treated in a condescending manner. I have no sense that women are treated as second-class citizens and that our work is not taken seriously.... We are not shoved off to marginal or minor committees.... The year I came in they hired five faculty; three of those were filled with women.* (Tierney & Bensimon, 1996, p. 94).

Creating positive climates for female faculty requires chairs who are sensitive to the personal lives of women, have a strong commitment to equity, and the determination to recruit not just one but a critical mass of women (in some cases a critical mass might be three, in others ten, 20, or more, depending on the size of the department). The following are specific ways in which chairs can create departments where women are intellectually valued and respected as professionals.

• Invite women faculty to share their work with the chair and provide feedback.

- Praise women faculty for their accomplishments; e.g., noticing when they receive positive evaluations, when they are awarded a grant, or an article they have written is published.

- Be understanding of special circumstances and provide assistance when possible. For example, many women academics are in commuting relationships and may require their chair's assistance in arranging schedules that facilitate their commute. Female assistant professors may be of childbearing age and special arrangements may need to be made for a family leave of absence.

- Refuse to give women assignments that can be stereotyped as "women's work" (e.g., planning departmental parties, getting coffee, baking a cake for a birthday). Certainly there are times when women will opt to do these activities, but chairs should not assume or suggest that women do so.

A department that treats all its members with respect and understanding will logically lead to greater collegiality and integration.

RACIAL AND ETHNIC MINORITIES AND COLLEGIALITY

> *In terms of other faculty of color, I think that there may be experiences that are unique to us, you know, our experiences of going through a graduate program as the only black person and our experiences dealing with the world at large. "Yes, you have a PhD. Yes, you know you have an education, you have gotten the highest degree that you can attain, and YES, WE'RE STILL TREATED LIKE NOBODIES." I don't think a white instructor could feel what it is like. This is something that I can talk about with other black faculty.* (Tierney & Bensimon, 1996, p. 119).

One of the most difficult problems encountered by racial and ethnic minorities is the burden of being the only one, knowing that their colleagues, regardless of how liberal-minded they might be, have neither the experiences nor, unfortunately, the need to understand what it feels like to be the "outsider within" or how these feelings influence their academic experience. The ideal solution to this problem is to hire faculty with the specific intent of increasing the racial and ethnic diversity of departments and institutions; however, few institutions have the capacity, the strategy, the policies, or the boldness that is required (Tierney & Bensimon, 1996). More often than not, when a department recruits a minority faculty member, this new person is recruited into a predominantly or all-white department. Just as the predominate maleness of a department is more likely to be noticed by women, the same is true in the case of minorities: They will be more acutely aware of a department's whiteness than their colleagues. In all likelihood, the department chair is also white, and being unaccustomed to thinking of the department in terms of race or gender, the chair can easily overlook his or her role in creating a climate that is responsive to minority faculty.

To accomplish the creation of academic climates that enable minorities to succeed, department chairs need to:

- **Be color-conscious.** Contrary to the commonly held belief that being colorblind ensures equal treatment, we suggest that in order to create academic departments and institutions that are welcoming of minority academics, department chairs must be uncommonly conscious of the racial and gender composition of their departments and their possible effects on minority newcomers (Tierney & Bensimon, 1996).

To claim that everyone is treated the same means not to recognize the double burden of being junior and minority, or the fact that minority faculty may not have had the socialization experiences that lead to successful integration in the academic profession. For example, while the advice to network may be valuable to a young professor who, as a graduate student, had opportunities to observe and participate in activities and projects that increased his or her cultural knowledge about how to manage an academic career, such advice may not be much use to someone who has not benefited from mentoring and does not possess a foundation from which to initiate a networking strategy. The fact that minority faculty have fewer professional socialization opportunities as graduate students has been extensively documented; therefore, it is incumbent on department chairs to consider more formal and structured ways of facilitating networking opportunities. Being color-conscious also means understanding why an action that may appear innocent can be interpreted as a hostile act when it involves a minority faculty member. For instance, a department chair who forgets to mention the first faculty meeting to a newly hired African-American professor is not only a poor administrator but also oblivious to how his oversight magnifies the outsider status of minority faculty.

- **Be conscious of institutionalized racism.** The alienation of minority faculty is more likely to be caused not by overt acts of bigotry and racism, but rather by the combination of attitudes, practices, and values that, despite not being racially motivated, nevertheless have the effect of producing and perpetuating inequities in the academy (Tierney & Bensimon, 1996).

  Department chairs need to understand the myriad ways in which the taken-for-granted, ostensibly race-neutral practices within a department can have a discriminatory impact on minority faculty. Common examples of institutionalized racism include judging scholarship that is minority-centered as ideological or political, disparaging publications that appear in minority based journals (e.g., the *Journal of Negro Education*), acts of omission, the failure to recruit minority students and scholars, the failure to generate hiring criteria more appropriate to the pool of minority scholars, social networks of the faculty that generally exclude people of color, and monocultural norms of success (Chesler & Crowfoot, 1989). A common manifestation of institutional racism is the failure of chairs and senior faculty to advocate inclusiveness and champion increased diversity. This failure places minority assistant professors in the uncomfortable and demoralizing position of becoming the sole spokespersons for minority interests. Additionally, when minority faculty become the lone voices on behalf of affirmative action on search or admissions committees, they risk being in conflict with senior colleagues on whose support they depend (Tierney & Bensimon, 1996).

- **Concentrate on retention.** The efforts that are put into wooing minority candidates often do not transfer over to the development of retention strategies, a situation which contributes to an unusually high rate of turnover among minority academics. Undoubtedly, the most critical quality for good leadership vis-a-vis the retention of minority faculty is providing them with a thorough understanding of the requirements for tenure and promotion and the resources to succeed.

- **Be aware of cultural taxation.** The term "cultural taxation" describes the obligation placed on minority faculty to help the institution represent diversity by serving on committees or by being expected to participate in a variety of activities that assistant professors may not normally carry out. The activities that typify cultural taxation are not likely to be rewarded; in fact, for faculty in institutions where scholarship is valued, such activities are likely to be detrimental. Nevertheless, minority faculty often feel or are made to feel that if they do not participate in these activities they are undermining the institution's diversity efforts, or they may feel a personal responsibility to, for instance, be available to counsel minority students (Tierney & Bensimon, 1996).

Department chairs can use their position and authority to protect minority academics from being overused by the institution or by their own sense of obligation. The critical role for the department chair is minimizing the requests that come to the minority faculty member for service activities and also taking a proactive stance and saying "no" on behalf of the professor who may not feel secure enough to do so.

Collegiality is a term that is often used in relation to departmental life, but one that is often misunderstood and elusive to new faculty. Some departments are fortunate that a natural flow of connection and friendly relations exist among their faculty without overt attempts made by the chair. In these departments, people get along, contribute to departmental decisions, work together, and enjoy interactions with one another. Other departments, however, struggle to include all their members in their functioning and are comprised of people who are highly individualistic and disinterested in departmental affairs. Department chairs who are proactive in assessing their departmental cultures for collegiality can take steps to encourage positive faculty interaction and create an environment that is more welcoming to new faculty.

We conclude this chapter with five checklists: One identifies behaviors that enable mentoring, one looks at behaviors that disable and shut down mentoring relationships, and another offers a brief look at how to establish good mentoring programs in your department. The final two checklists provide methods for measuring and promoting departmental collegiality.

CHECKLIST: ENABLING MENTORING BEHAVIOR

☐ Shares grant opportunities and calls for papers with junior faculty

☐ Offers advice in an approachable manner

☐ Invites casual discussions of issues in teaching, service, research, and tenure review

☐ Routinely volunteers to visit junior colleagues' classrooms to offer advice or to write a letter for the tenure file

☐ Visits junior faculty in their offices for friendly chats.

☐ Provides junior faculty with information about preparing for tenure review

CHECKLIST: DISABLING MENTORING BEHAVIOR

☐ Expects junior faculty to make the initial contact

☐ Assumes all is well unless there is a complaint

☐ Requires new faculty to do things the chair's way

☐ Never chats with new faculty on their turf

☐ Refuses to visit faculty classrooms

CHECKLIST: ESTABLISHING A MENTORING PROGRAM

☐ Show concern for each faculty member's development.

☐ Serve as a role model.

☐ Support program development opportunities.

☐ Promote faculty activities and accomplishments.

☐ Provide special opportunities for skill development.

Checklist: Assessing Levels of Collegiality

- ☐ Do junior and senior, new and existing faculty routinely interact?
- ☐ Are relations in the department strained or cordial?
- ☐ Do faculty collaborate on projects?
- ☐ Do faculty coteach courses?
- ☐ Are there faculty who are excluded from departmental interactions?
- ☐ Are there faculty who are excluded from departmental gatherings?
- ☐ Are there cliques of faculty that either purposefully or mistakenly exclude others?
- ☐ Do any faculty in the department feel left out?
- ☐ Are decisions for the department made by only a few of the faculty?
- ☐ Are there important things happening in the department that some faculty are not aware of?

Checklist: Fostering Collegiality

- ☐ Create ample opportunity for faculty to come together both formally and informally.
- ☐ Plan one activity (e.g., colloquia, lunch) at least once per month during the academic year that includes and welcomes all faculty.
- ☐ Financially support opportunities for team teaching.
- ☐ Encourage collaboration between junior and senior faculty.
- ☐ Equally inform all faculty about important departmental decisions.
- ☐ Act as a role model for inclusive interactions with your faculty.
- ☐ Encourage constructive disagreement among faculty.

REFERENCES

Boice, R. (1992). *The new faculty member: Supporting and fostering professional development.* San Francisco, CA: Jossey-Bass.

Chesler, M. A., & Crowfoot, J. E.. (1989). *Racism in higher education.* Ann Arbor, MI: University of Michigan.

Gmelch, W. H., & Miskin, V. D. (1995). *Chairing an academic department.* Thousand Oaks, CA: Sage.

Neumann, A. (1993, April). *The ties that bind: Notes on professorial colleagueship as academic context.* American Educational Research Association.

Tierney, W. G., & Bensimon, E. M. (1996). *Promotion and tenure: Community and socialization in academe.* Albany, NY: SUNY Press.

Whitt, E. J. (1991). Hit the ground running: Experiences of new faculty in a school of education. *Review of Higher Education, 14*(2), 177-197.

CHAPTER 11

DEMYSTIFYING THE PROMOTION AND TENURE PROCESS

When I was hired I was given a packet of papers to complete to accompany my review. In my second year review, I thought I was prepared, but found the rules of the game changing. I am constantly getting mixed messages. My department chair told me not to worry about research and service until my third year. He recommends that I focus on my teaching to get started. The people at the college level and above tell me to focus on my research and make it known that we (tenure-track faculty) need to do our share of committee work. I'm squeezed between these expectations among different levels of administrators.

It is so hard to know what to do to achieve tenure. The guidelines are not clearly stated at the outset, and depending on whom I talk to, they constantly change.

Department chair involvement is key to helping junior faculty balance expectations for the tenure process. New faculty need to know the relative importance of the criteria for promotion and tenure at the department, college, and institutional levels. By knowing faculty histories and seeking to understand their needs, department chairs can anticipate ways to facilitate individual faculty success and act as junior faculty advocates. This chapter addresses the department chair's role in the promotion and tenure process, including the importance of talking with junior faculty about the relative weights of teaching, research, and service, and the review process itself. Stress and time conflicts are inherent to the tenure process; thus, we also focus on how department chairs can help junior faculty manage these difficulties.

One of the greatest stresses for junior faculty, as exemplified in the comments at the outset of this section, is the lack of and conflicting information about the promotion and tenure process. While orientation programs and faculty handbooks typically provide new faculty with general information about promotion and tenure (as discussed in Part II), they often fall short in preparing faculty for specific information to negotiate the tenure process itself. New faculty in search of successful tenure know they need to demonstrate ability and success in the areas of research, teaching, and service. However, what constitutes ability or success or even research is often unclear.

Such confusion as described in the excerpts above can be dissipated by the department chair's clarification of the nuances of the tenure process and by becoming aware of the advice others are giving the new faculty about tenure expectations at that institution. There is nothing more confusing or stressful for the new faculty member than receiving conflicting information from various sources. Department chairs play a key role in helping new faculty determine what is a "rule," whether formal or informal, and what is just one person's interpretation of policy. What can department chairs do to alleviate such confusion and stress?

MECHANISMS FOR SUCCESS

The department chair must have a comprehensive understanding of the subtleties of the tenure process at all levels of the institution and be willing to relay that knowledge to all new faculty. New faculty members may make assumptions about tenure expectations based on very little information. These institutional and departmental expectations should be clearly articulated from the beginning of the junior faculty member's employment. While it may not be possible to provide tenure-track faculty with the level of "cookbook" detail they would like, department chairs, with the support of other senior faculty, must take care not to withhold useful information. The lack of clear and pertinent information about promotion and tenure creates significant stress for some faculty and can impede socialization and progress toward tenure.

Campuses vary greatly in how they evaluate junior faculty. Some do annual reviews while others only do reviews at three years and then again in the final year to determine a tenure decision. Regardless of institutional policies for promotion and tenure reviews, department chairs can facilitate the progress and socialization of their junior faculty by meeting with them regularly to discuss promotion and tenure. For some chairs this may mean once a semester (e.g., when teaching evaluations are compiled) and for others once a year (e.g., before the dossier is due in the event of annual evaluations). Regardless, the intent of these meetings should be to explicitly talk about promotion and tenure guidelines and how the new faculty member is making progress. This is also an opportune time for department chairs to inform faculty about any changes in tenure guidelines as well as to discuss how to best prepare the faculty member for reviews. The biggest mistake a department chair can make is to let the new faculty member know how they are doing on the tenure track after the review has taken place. Reviews, whether conducted annually or at two-year intervals, are inherently stressful. Department chairs can help circumvent this stress by taking a proactive position. The scenario that follows provides an example of a new faculty member who was not given the appropriate information on how to succeed at her institution.

Scenario: Clarice is a new tenure-track faculty member in the department of business administration. The college is considered a teaching institution; however, faculty are increasingly expected to be involved in producing research for publication. She has spent the past two years completing her dissertation and teaching introductory business courses in a community college. Other than her dissertation and work on a textbook for business students, her research experience is limited. Her dissertation is impressive, she writes well, and has plans for a research project with a faculty member from her previous institution. Clarice has excellent teaching evaluations and is highly recommended by her advisors.

Response: Clarice is in many ways a typical new faculty member: She shows promise as a scholar but is a fairly inexperienced researcher. Faculty need to be informed of research expectations, including information about appropriate journals, conference presentations, and grant funding agencies. Make it clear where faculty should be at certain points in their career so they do not fall behind and endanger their chances of receiving tenure.

Depending on the size of the department, the number of junior faculty in the unit, and other resources available on campus (e.g., a faculty development office), department chairs need to help faculty navigate the areas of teaching, research, and service, paying particular attention to the following questions (Rodrigues, 1993):

- What are teaching expectations in the department?

- How do faculty demonstrate teaching abilities?

- What are research expectations in the department?

- Are there certain publications where faculty are supposed to publish?

- How much service is enough?

Departmental cultures vary greatly on any given campus and within higher education as a whole. Department chairs serve their junior faculty well by addressing the above questions and ensuring that they remain on track to meet the expectations for teaching, research, and service. The following scenario illustrates how lack of information can lead junior faculty away from research activities.

Scenario: Jennifer puts all her energy into teaching and service-oriented activities and neglects sending papers to conferences or journals. She believes that her institution will reward her for her hard work, dedication to students, and the improved learning environment. At her fourth-year review, she is told that unless she publishes quite a bit in the next year, she will have no hope of being granted tenure at that institution.

Response: Give specific information about what counts in tenure decisions and follow up with yearly discussions with nontenured faculty to ensure they are addressing those guidelines in their work. Protect untenured faculty from heavy service obligations

Professor Robert Diamond (1995), instructional developer at Syracuse University, provides healthy advice for new faculty in his book *Preparing for Promotion and Tenure Review.* In this work, Diamond advises the new faculty member to begin preparing for the promotion and tenure review from the start of their position. We certainly agree and present some of Diamond's advice (pp. 4-6) in the following section to help chairs direct new faculty in successful promotion and tenure efforts.

HELPING NEW FACULTY LEARN THE ROPES:
WHAT FACULTY NEED TO KNOW

- **The review process in your unit.** Is there an annual review procedure? Is this a formal or informal review process? What is required? Is there a more comprehensive three-year review? How is it similar or different in process and practice from the tenure review?

- **The type of documentation the committee will expect.** What materials does the committee expect junior faculty to provide to document teaching, research, and service? If a portfolio is expected, what should be included? How should it be organized and presented? Will the faculty member have to submit actual copies of publications? Does the file need to include letters of support? If so, from whom? How many? Do faculty need to provide references?

- **The steps that committees follow to make promotion and tenure decisions.** What steps will the committee follow? What is the timeline? Will the committee interview colleagues and students about the candidate? Will documentation or assessment be solicited outside the institution? Is there an external review process? Do junior faculty know how to best pick these reviewers?

- **The criteria that will be used to assess the quality of the materials that are provided.** How will publications be counted? Is the process weighted to differentiate among publications? What types of publications are valued in your department? How will quality teaching and advising be evaluated? How are professional activities measured?

- **The relative weighting of various activities.** Is there a set formula to determine the importance of particular materials submitted, or is this individually determined? Is there a particular approach to determining the relative weight of activities (e.g., 30% teaching, 30% research, 30% service)?

The department chair who addresses these types of questions will help the new faculty member prepare a dossier that is comprehensive and more likely to succeed. By going into the review process prepared with answers to the above questions, junior faculty can prioritize and organize their workload and professional activities accordingly (Diamond, 1995).

A WORD ABOUT STRESS

We close this chapter with a discussion about stress because it is endemic to the promotion and tenure process, especially in the first three years of an academic appointment (Pugh & Dinham, 1997). Stress largely emanates from the unwritten nuances of promotion and tenure as well as the difficulties of being in a new institution and, in many instances, a new geographic area. While junior faculty tend to be confident as teachers, researchers, and contributing members of their disciplines and institutions, stress is still a major factor in dealing with the uncertainties that surround questions such as How much teaching? Where should my research be published? and What types of service are valued? Earlier we addressed the department chair's role in directly addressing these types of questions. We now turn to some suggestions department chairs can offer junior faculty as they encounter the inherent uncertainties (read: stress) of the tenure track.

Common Stressors

Based on a review of the literature on tenure-track faculty and our interviews with faculty from across the country, the following is a list of stresses identified by junior faculty:

Personal and professional conflicts
- Lack of time to perform well professionally and to have a fulfilling personal life

- Conflicts between professional and personal spheres

- Finding a balanced schedule

- Balancing work and family demands

- Knowing how much is too much talk about family and other personal matters

Promotion and tenure concerns
- Lack of time to complete tasks perceived as necessary to achieve tenure

- Decoding promotion and tenure guidelines (i.e., figuring out what is really required for promotion and tenure)

- Knowing how much research, teaching, and service is the right balance

- The review process

- Guilt if not working (scholarly work can be endless)

- For women considering having children, conflicts between the tenure clock and the biological clock

- Difficulty with getting a lab started or other research materials when the tenure clock is running

- Change in leadership either on promotion and tenure committees or in the chair, dean, or provost position, resulting in changed tenure expectations

- Uncertainty about mission and purpose of institution (e.g., an institution with a focus on teaching, but push for research when tenure is reviewed)

Teaching issues
- Classroom concerns (e.g., evaluations, discipline, preparing the right amount of material)

- Feeling like a fraud

- Excessive student demands

Faculty and departmental concerns
- Negotiating departmental politics

- Feeling unable to say "no" to service requests (especially an issue for women and people of color who may be the only one who can represent the department in terms of race and/or gender)

- Knowing when it is okay to say "no"

- Competition among junior faculty and/or between junior and senior faculty who often operate under different sets of expectations

- Not having the support expected when hired for the position

- Figuring out a balance between collaboration and individual work

- Generational differences between senior and junior faculty, old-timers and newcomers

- Isolation

- Lack of collegiality

- Dealing with a chilly climate (particularly for women and people of color in departments that historically have been predominantly male and white)

- A research agenda that is considered nonmainstream (again, this can be a particular stress for faculty of color who are often hired to do research in areas that are not considered mainstream, but then have to deal with the stress of not fitting in)

- Uncertainty and fear about the future

- Departmental conflicts

- Not knowing where to turn for help and support

What we see when we look at this list are several personal, professional, and procedural conflicts. But is it the department chair's role to address issues of stress and anxiety? Certainly new faculty must take some responsibility for their own stresses, but given the changing nature of promotion and tenure on most campuses and the large number of faculty entering the ranks of the tenure track, we believe it is crucial for department chairs to find ways to address stress-related issues, whether personal or professional. Further, department chairs play a role in setting a tone in the unit that can either spark or suppress stress.

Ultimately, the faculty member who is able to find relief from the types of anxieties mentioned above will be a much more productive member of the department. Institutional responses to junior faculty stress will not only help the junior faculty member, but also the institution as it seeks to build a productive faculty. Below we discuss some steps chairs can take to help junior faculty find ways to cope with stress.

Developing a personal interest and an ethic of caring will help faculty know they have someone to turn to when they need support. This is not to suggest that chairs must take on the stresses of every new faculty member, but being aware of their stresses and finding the resources they need to combat them will help faculty overcome feelings of isolation and loneliness.

Department chairs need to be cognizant of junior faculty as people. Too often, professional and personal spheres get separated to the point of tension. This is not to suggest that new faculty should bring their children with them to work everyday, but it is important for department chairs to realize that new faculty have many facets to their lives. The faculty member who feels as if she or he has to work all the time to keep up is likely to get burned out and/or to be very unhappy in the position.

Lack of time and stress go together. Junior faculty feel as if they never have enough time to complete what needs to be done. Department chairs can help junior faculty by reducing teaching and advising loads. Many departments offer new faculty course reductions in their first year. While this is helpful, a new position brings with it much adjustment, and so it may be unwise to use the course reduction to get other things done (e.g., research). For faculty at research institutions in particular, course reductions in years two or three on the tenure track can be very helpful to boost productivity.

Another source of stress relief for junior faculty are faculty development programs. These are great sources of support for new faculty but unfortunately, not all campuses have them. On campuses where these types of programs are not available, department chairs may want to consider teaming with other units to offer workshops that may be of help to new faculty across campus.

In the next chapter we focus on the department chair's role in developing effective researchers.

CHECKLIST: HELPING WITH STRESS MANAGEMENT

☐ Get to know faculty, their interests, and their concerns.

☐ Look at the whole person.

☐ Clearly articulate expectations for promotion and tenure.

☐ Focus on development and socialization of new faculty.

☐ Develop discussion groups for new faculty to share mutual concerns.

☐ Help junior faculty find mentors for support.

☐ Negotiate reduced teaching loads for junior faculty.

☐ Connect faculty with resources available beyond the department.

CHECKLIST: ELIMINATING PROMOTION AND TENURE CONFUSION

☐ Impart explicit written information about university, college, and department standards for promotion and tenure.

☐ Meet regularly with junior faculty to go over progress toward tenure.

☐ Devise mechanisms to help junior faculty monitor progress in teaching, research, and service.

REFERENCES

Diamond, R. M. (1995). *Preparing for promotion and tenure review: A faculty guide.* Bolton, MA: Anker.

Pugh, K. L., & Dinham, S. M. (1997). *The structure of stress in newly hired junior faculty.* Paper presented at the annual meeting of the American Educational Research Association. Chicago, IL.

Rodrigues, R. J. (1993, Summer). Translating your department culture for junior faculty. *The Department Chair: A Newsletter for Academic Administrators, (4)* 1, 9-10.

CHAPTER 12

Developing Productive Researchers

I'm good at research, and I like it. My advisor encouraged me to apply to a research school, and this department is the best in the country. They have the resources for me to start up a lab and to have a graduate student assistant. That's important for a research program. I'm happy here. I probably spend 30% of my time writing grants, 30% of my time in the lab and doing research, 30% teaching, and another 30% on service and department stuff. Yeah, I know. I'm busy!

It has never been laid out too clearly for me. For example, if you have one single-author article in a top journal that everybody cites and then a whole lot of secondary stuff, is that enough? Or if you have five or six pretty good articles in secondary or specialty journals, is that enough? Is that equivalent to having one really great article and a whole lot of book chapters? Do you have to have a book?

I thought that my review packet was completed, but then at the last minute new forms were given out that mentioned criteria I had never heard of. Needless to say, I found this to be extremely anxiety producing.

The person who made the first comment above clearly values research highly, so he chose an institution with the same values. Not all new faculty can make such a good match, and not all institutions are so clear about their research and other expectations. Research expectations can present a lot of angst for the new tenure-track faculty member because institutions vary considerably in their expectations, as illustrated in the last two excerpts above. However, we do know that research is the most rewarded of all faculty activities regardless of institutional type and, as previously discussed, it is also a great source of stress for junior faculty.

This section seeks to address the department chair's role in developing effective researchers by exploring the following questions: What can department chairs do to help newcomers pursue an effective research agenda? What are some of the most common problems junior faculty have with research, and how can department chairs help solve those problems? What are some of the special issues with regard to women and minorities? How can you, as a department chair, recognize a productive junior faculty member?

FINDING A BALANCE

We start with quotes from three faculty members all exhibiting what Robert Boice (1992) refers to as "busyness."

> *I just am too involved in teaching. I am a little bit concerned, but not too much, because I know that I can write, but I am having a hard time balancing. I get really involved in the teaching, and then I get kind of overwhelmed with all the daily details and my writing comes last. I am afraid I spend too much time teaching. I am going to have to cut back . . . I am not going to have all lower level courses do a field research project.*

> *The first year I spent teaching and settling in and getting my life together because that is what everybody told me to do. Now I wish I had that year back. I would have backed off my teaching a little bit, and not spent so much time preparing for classes.*

> *I wish I could learn how to organize my time; then I could spend more time writing. The unknown here for me is the scholarship, in terms of how much I can produce while teaching.*

As Boice points out, faculty who do not develop into scholars are those who lack a research agenda, have few publications, have negative attitudes toward writing, have high levels of perfectionism, justify limited writing output to higher personal standards, typically take a long time to finish their dissertations, and have few or no publications when they start out in their academic career. While the expectations for being a productive scholar and researcher vary according to institutional type, department chairs should try to make expectations more clear. This can be done in a variety of ways:

- Telling new faculty that studies of faculty productivity and patterns of success for new faculty reveal an unstated expectation for faculty to publish between one and one and a half articles per year during the probationary period

- Helping new faculty develop productive habits

Boice found that unproductive faculty tend to attribute their poor performance to lack of time, that they must have large chunks of time to write. Contrary to this widely held belief, Boice suggests that individuals who find brief periods to write (e.g., one or two hours, three or four days a week) as part of a consistent regimen will be more productive than those who feel they cannot write unless they have blocks of uninterrupted time. If we think that writing can only be done on Fridays or on the weekend when we are able to sit in front of the computer from 8:00 a.m. to 8:00 p.m., and do not write on any other days, it is difficult to maintain a consistent rhythm.

The goal for department chairs is to help new faculty establish a regular schedule for writing, and perhaps the best advice that chairs can give new faculty is to be more conscious of time management. Just as they are able to schedule appointments to advise students or to meet with a colleague, they should also make writing appointments that are treated with the same seriousness as one might treat an appointment with another human being. Department chairs play a role in maintaining this regime by encouraging faculty to find a schedule that works for them (e.g., writing 8:00 to 10:00 a.m., Monday, Wednesday, Friday) and then supporting faculty in these efforts by honoring this schedule.

Chairs can also be supportive by helping new faculty develop the characteristics and habits that researchers such as Boice (1992) and Bland and Schmitz (1986) identify with productive researchers:

- They are very involved in the campus and have been successful in establishing collaborative and mentoring relationships.

- They spend about five hours per week building collegiality for themselves, through face-to-face visits, letters, phone calls, and email. Professional networks enable faculty to build their knowledge base, to read prepublished manuscripts, and to have their work reviewed.

- They establish productive scholarly habits early in their careers. Research on faculty productivity suggests that unless such habits take hold within the first five years of a junior faculty member's appointment, they are unlikely to be developed later (Bland & Schmitz, 1986).

- They have positive attitudes toward the campus, colleagues, and students (Boice, 1992).

- They spend two hours of teaching preparation per classroom hour. They have learned how to use varied methods of teaching, including lecturing and eliciting student participation (Boice, 1992).

- They are engaged in multiple simultaneous projects (e.g., collecting data, writing articles on completed research), so that they are buffered from disappointment if not all their activities succeed (Bland & Schmitz, 1986).

- They have in-depth knowledge of their research area.

- They are familiar with all major published works in their area, current major projects being conducted, different theories, key researchers, and predominant funding sources (Bland & Schmitz, 1986).

Faculty who fail to establish effective research and writing skills early in their career reduce the likelihood of promotion and tenure.

STEPS TO HELPING FACULTY ESTABLISH AND MAINTAIN A RESEARCH AGENDA

In addition to the tips offered above, based on our research and review of the literature on faculty development, we provide steps that department chairs can take to help faculty establish and maintain a research agenda. Although our discussion is geared toward tenure-track faculty, these suggestions are applicable to revitalize the research of tenured faculty as well.

Step 1: Know the Research History

At the time of hire, familiarize yourself with the new faculty member's research history. Does the new faculty member have an established research agenda? Is he currently involved in research projects? What kind of publication record does she have? Such an assessment will help determine how much help the new faculty member needs to establish a research agenda. Some faculty may need more direction than the new faculty member who has a history of grant acquisition and scholarly publication.

Step 2: Help Create a Research Agenda

Tenure-track faculty, and, in particular, first-time faculty, need direction to start and maintain a research agenda. For faculty who have a research plan established, the department chair may simply need to meet with them to assess how feasible the agenda is and to determine if it will contribute to a successful tenure decision. Other faculty are likely to have ideas about what they plan to do in terms of research, but are not sure how to implement the agenda. Faculty with limited research experience will need one-to-one assistance from the chair to talk about designing and establishing a research agenda compatible with the faculty member's needs and the institution's expectations for tenure. The scenario below illustrates how a new faculty member may need help making the transition from graduate student to professor.

Scenario: Deborah has finished her dissertation and started a new position as an assistant professor. Her only publication credits are articles conceived of and written by her thesis advisor. She has thoughts of revising her dissertation—or parts of it—for publication, but what to cut and what to expand upon isn't completely clear, and she doesn't know where to send her work even if it was publishable. She has never applied for a grant for her research although her dissertation was based on data funded by grants her dissertation advisor was awarded.

Response: Link faculty early on with senior researcher(s) with similar interests who will incorporate the junior faculty into the network of the field and offer pertinent information about publishing and grant-writing strategies.

Step 3: Meet Regularly about Research

Regular meetings with new faculty provide both the department chair and the new faculty member with ample opportunity to learn expectations for research in the department and at the institution. Such meetings help to create collegiality and can ensure that the new faculty member is not shocked at annual review time.

Scenario: New faculty have difficulty meeting ambiguous expectations as the tenure process progresses. In a department that ranked publications according to whether they appeared in "first tier," "second tier," or "third tier" journals, and earn a negative grade if they appear in a "glossy publication with a picture of the author," Maria still found the criteria hard to decipher. What is meant by "significant, meaningful research?"

Response: Meet regularly (at least twice yearly) to monitor the faculty's progress and to reiterate department and university expectations for tenure. Provide sample dossiers or portfolios from recently tenured colleagues who were successful throughout the promotion and tenure review process. Help junior colleagues understand how to interpret review letters and requirements.

Step 4: Pinpoint Problems

Based on regular meetings with junior faculty, department chairs may see specific problem areas. For example, a director of a faculty development program identified a need to enhance the writing productivity of new faculty. She organized a writing group for faculty with the goal of providing a structured arena for taking a manuscript from start to publication. The group provides a model that department chairs can use to help faculty with their writing productivity. Again, calling upon Boice's research on establishing and maintaining scholarly productivity, we provide the following writing tips department chairs can offer their faculty. Moody (1997) also offers useful tips.

- *Make writing a moderate, not escalated, priority.* Incorporate writing into daily activities and try to avoid writing during evenings, weekends, and vacations. Try to produce something every day even if it is small (e.g., writing notes) whether you feel like it or not.

- *Write when you are fresh.* For most people this is in the morning. It also helps to keep a log or chart of writing activities that shows your

writing schedule and what you actually did. Start with small incre-
ments of time (10–15 minutes) and build up to a block of time that
feels comfortable (an hour or so). Avoid spending large chunks of
time on writing so you don't overdo it.

- *Compliment and reward yourself when you meet daily goals.* Positive
  self talk is empowering. As you establish a comfortable writing routine, consider working on a couple different projects at once. This
  will help with the cross-fertilization of ideas.

- *Establish or get into a writing support group.* If it is difficult to maintain a regular writing schedule, a group of fellow faculty can help to
  develop and maintain positive writing habits.

- *Get into the habit of sharing work with colleagues even if it is in outline or draft form.* This will help de-emphasize the private side of
  writing and will establish a network of colleagues who get to know
  and support your work. Making work public is also a great way to
  build a list of external reviewers who, if called upon, will be familiar
  with your work.

- *Develop a portfolio of research that includes completed projects, writing in progress, and plans for the future.* The portfolio can become a
  discussion piece for annual reviews and meetings with department
  chairs and colleagues. Further, the portfolio is a means to assess the
  development of a coherent research agenda and to monitor areas that
  need to be developed.

Step 5: Help with Grant Proposals

The department chair should work with the faculty member who is having
difficulty getting grant applications accepted. This is especially important
at institutions where there are expectations for productivity in this area.
Too often, faculty are not explicitly aware of what they are expected to
accomplish with regard to external funding. Department chairs can aid
faculty in grant acquisition by showing the faculty member an example of
a recently accepted grant application and providing feedback on drafts of
his or her grant proposals.

If more than one faculty member is having difficulty with the same
issue, schedule a topical workshop. For example, a grant writing workshop,
like "ins and outs of the grant writing process," would be helpful. Invite a
speaker with experience and success in grant writing to provide tips and

advice as well as feedback on individual faculty member's proposal drafts. This may be an area where department chairs can tap into campus-based resources. Research administration or faculty development offices, if available, may conduct grant writing workshops. If so, department chairs can recommend attendance for faculty and then provide follow-up support to move ideas into proposals.

Step 6: Support Research Interests

Nontenured faculty who are interested in cutting-edge research or research into sensitive areas may feel that they are not free to pursue those interests because of the reaction of the tenure and promotion committee. If faculty are hired to support research in a particular area, chairs need to support these interests. The following scenario offers an example of such a dilemma.

Scenario: Chris's research methodology is based on lesbian feminist theory. Her institution is conservative and in the past has awarded tenure to faculty in very traditional research arenas. Chris was hired by her department to cover the growing interest in feminist topics and alternative lifestyle issues in her field. She worries that her research interests may prevent her from being awarded tenure.

Response: Be an advocate for the legitimate research interests of your faculty. Monitor promotion and tenure reviews of faculty to detect such prejudices from colleagues.

The steps that we offer for aiding junior faculty in their research agenda may be shared by chairs and mentors, but it is important that they not be neglected. Being successful, productive researchers is still the key to promotion and tenure at most institutions, and responsible chairs will help to create an atmosphere conducive to productivity for their nontenured faculty.

The suggestions we have offered throughout this chapter are geared toward the ongoing development of the junior faculty member. The tenure process typically lasts five to seven years depending on the institution. It is important for department chairs to be actively involved in focused junior faculty development throughout the entire tenure process. In the next chapter, we focus on continuing the development of junior faculty as teachers.

CHECKLIST: ESTABLISHING A RESEARCH AGENDA

☐ Assess the level of involvement needed to encourage research productivity.

☐ Work with faculty to develop a research agenda.

☐ Meet with faculty regularly.

☐ Identify problem areas and provide potential solutions.

☐ Help the new faculty member with grant applications.

☐ Support nontraditional research areas.

REFERENCES

Bland, C. J., & Schmitz, D. (1986). Characteristics of the successful researcher: Implications for faculty development. *Journal of Medical Education, 61* (1).

Boice, R. (1992). *The new faculty member: Supporting and fostering professional development.* San Francisco, CA: Jossey-Bass.

Moody, J. (1997). *Demystifying the profession: Helping junior faculty succeed.* New Haven, CT: University of New Haven Press.

Tierney, W. G., & Bensimon, E. M. (1996). *Promotion and tenure: Community and socialization in academe.* Albany, NY: SUNY Press.

CHAPTER 13

DEVELOPING EFFECTIVE TEACHERS

I was completely unprepared for the teaching philosophy that is used here. I found that very stressful and quite disturbing. I teach large classes, large in terms of this institution's standards, 50 to 60 students. And I was getting the message that teaching takes place through a very interactive approach, a discussion-oriented approach, and not a lecture-oriented approach, and I was struggling to implement that in my classes. And, in many cases, I internalized that pressure of the expectations and how you teach here, so that created stress for me. Where I had taught before, I had primarily used a very lecture-oriented approach, and I had no problems; there was plenty of discussion because students were excited and interested. Here, I found it much more difficult. I had to structure the interaction much more and put more forethought into it. It didn't just occur. And so I felt very stressed by what I perceived as my initial inability to meet the expectations of what is considered good teaching here. But with time it has gone away.

———————

Before I got here my teaching experience was limited to my teaching assistantship in graduate school. I helped teach two introductory courses. The courses were large lectures, so I thought I could handle teaching the same when I got here, even though my teaching responsibilities were with small break-out sessions. I observed the professor I worked with in graduate school and assumed I would use some of the same strategies he did. I mostly relied on lectures because I thought that was the only way to teach a semester's worth of material to over 150 students. I thought things were going okay, but was shocked when I got my teaching evaluations back. Students didn't feel like they got good instruction or good information. Now I'm freaked out because my teaching assignment for fall still includes that class, and I'm at a loss as to what to do to cover all the material with such a large group of students.

In view of the rising concern with the quality of teaching, the increasing emphasis on student evaluations, and the extent to which faculty are able to incorporate new methods and involve students in research projects, it is important that department chairs provide new faculty with the resources to be successful in the classroom. As exemplified in the second excerpt above, it takes time to develop new faculty into effective teachers. Most new faculty graduate from research institutions where the priority is on research, yet the majority of positions held by new faculty are in teaching-oriented institutions. Therefore, department chairs cannot rely on past socialization to prepare faculty for their teaching roles. Instead, they must take a proactive stance to develop junior faculty into effective teachers. The purpose of this chapter is to address the department chair's role in helping new faculty develop as teachers. We provide suggestions for department chairs to prepare faculty for their role as teachers, dealing with the multiple roles of teaching, diverse classrooms, student evaluations, and incorporating teaching into promotion and tenure reviews.

As shown in the first excerpt above, smaller teaching-centered institutions frequently have distinctive philosophies about teaching and learning and expect newcomers to adopt them. The role of the department chair in such cases is to reduce the stress that the individual might experience in making the transition from their graduate program's culture of research to the employing institution's culture of teaching. If the department chair is concerned about the quality of teaching and teaching is a "real" priority (i.e., it is taken seriously in the evaluation of faculty for promotion and tenure), then the department chair can be influential in developing new faculty into excellent teachers. We begin by addressing the definition of effective teaching.

What Is Effective Teaching?

There is no one best instructional method. What makes for effective instruction varies by student, class, content, and discipline. Based on research and practice regarding teaching, Davis (1993, *xix-xx*) identifies four clusters of skills, strategies, and attitudes that promote students' academic achievement.

1) **Organizing and explaining material in ways appropriate to students' abilities.** Effective teaching involves the instructor's understanding of content knowledge and the ability to convey that knowledge to students. Effective instruction calls upon teachers to gauge student backgrounds and learning styles in order to use appropriate methods to explain difficult concepts.

2) **Creating an environment for learning.** Effective instruction calls for teachers to establish rapport with students. Further, it involves responding to students' needs, communicating high expectations, giving feedback, and respecting student diversity and ways of learning. Good teachers emphasize cooperation, collaboration, and other modes of active learning.

3) **Helping students become autonomous, self-regulated learners.** Effective teachers communicate course goals and expectations, help students establish their own connections to course content, view learning collaboratively, and stimulate students' intellectual interest.

4) **Reflect on and evaluate teaching.** Good teachers invest time in examining why they do what they do and how that affects student learning. Effective instruction calls for continuous reflection and improvement.

Common to these four clusters of skills is reflective practice—effective teachers, and the department chairs who support them, spend time thinking about teaching and strive to continuously improve their practice. Department chairs can create a culture of effective teaching by talking about teaching regularly, supporting and rewarding good teaching, helping junior faculty become good teachers, recognizing that most good teachers are made and not born that way, and spending time helping faculty to find their niche as teachers.

PREPARING FACULTY FOR THEIR ONGOING ROLES AS TEACHERS

For the new faculty member, the first year in the classroom means finding ways to balance classroom and student demands with other faculty responsibilities. Beyond the first year, faculty need to find ways to integrate their roles as teachers, scholars, and institutional citizens. The teaching role, although not always the most rewarded, is certainly the most public of all faculty duties. Getting a college education represents a major financial investment for parents, students, and taxpayers. And while a college education is not only desirable but increasingly necessary, there is also a greater expectation from parents and taxpayers that the quality of instruction justifies the increasing costs of college tuition.

In the last few years, colleges and universities have begun to pay greater attention to teaching. Even in research universities where teaching is typically secondary to research, there is greater scrutiny of teaching performance. The majority of new faculty have not had any formal preparation on how to be a college teacher and may have very little knowledge as to how they impact the quality of undergraduate education in their department and institution. Many of the teaching and advisement mistakes that new faculty make, though they may appear to result from indifference and lack of caring, really stem from lack of preparation and ignorance of the research on teaching and learning.

It is crucial that department chairs be familiar with the conditions associated with student learning and develop faculty expertise in order to facilitate those conditions. Recent research on good practices in undergraduate education have identified several attributes of a quality undergraduate education. We briefly discuss these below and provide suggestions on how chairs can actively work to help new faculty embrace these practices and make them part of their teaching repertoire.

HELPING FACULTY IMPROVE AS TEACHERS

Here we provide ten practices that chairs can implement to help faculty improve classroom learning, comfort with teaching, and student evaluations.

1) **Set high expectations and make active efforts to help students meet them.** New faculty need to learn how to set high but attainable expectations and be able to communicate them clearly to students at the start of a course (ECS, 1996).

2) **Develop respect for diverse talents and learning styles.** Students come to college with vastly different backgrounds, levels of preparation, and previous experiences. New faculty have to learn how to design curricula and courses to meet diverse backgrounds (ECS, 1996).

3) **The freshman year is critical to student success.** New faculty need to be aware that what happens to first-year students in their classes can have long lasting effects on student motivation and retention (ECS, 1996; Light, 1992).

4) **Assignments should emphasize the development of higher order skills.** New faculty need to learn strategies to incorporate activities and projects designed to strengthen students' critical thinking, effective written and oral communication, and problem solving (ECS, 1996).

5) **Effective teaching fosters active learning.** Students learn best when they are given multiple opportunities to actively exercise and demonstrate skills. Chairs can help new faculty learn how to combine lecturing with discussion, create assignments that apply learned material to new settings and contexts, and assess student performance on the basis of application rather than exclusively on recall.

6) **Faculty need to offer regular assessment and prompt feedback.** Student learning is enhanced when students are provided with information about their performance promptly and frequently. This feedback can be done both within courses and through advising. Students need to know where they stand with their course material.

7) **Collaboration helps learning.** Students learn better when engaged in a team effort. Collaboration reinforces communication and problem solving skills. Richard Light's (1992) work at Harvard revealed that the academic performance of students, as well as their satisfaction with college, are tied closely to involvement with other students around substantive work.

8) **Learning requires adequate time on task.** Students need time, both within class and out of class, to contemplate and complete assignments.

9) **Out-of-class contact with faculty enhances learning.** Frequency of academic out-of-class contact between faculty members and students is a strong determinant of both program completion and effective

learning. Knowing a few faculty members well from both in and out of class contact enhances students' intellectual commitment. Light's research confirms the interpersonal nature of academic involvement and academic success. He points out "that nearly every student who describes strong academic performance can point to a specific activity that ties academic work closely to another person or a group of people" (Light, 1992, p.18).

10) **Don't overload students with information.** It is better to have students learn less material well than for students to be overloaded with facts and principles and other information they cannot apply.

A central component to effective teaching is active learning that is centered around not only group work (both in and out of the classroom) but also collaboration and the sharing of ideas. What can new faculty, with the help of their department chairs, do to encourage collaboration and team approaches to learning in their classrooms?

FACILITATING INTERPERSONAL ENGAGEMENT AROUND ACADEMIC WORK

Faculty do well to provide simple guidelines for students on how to establish study groups. Guidelines can include suggestions for frequency of meetings, amount of time to meet, how to attain desired outcomes, pitfalls to watch out for, and how to handle unproductive group members. This is a particularly good strategy to bring about greater interpersonal engagement in large classrooms. Study groups can be used for students to prepare for tests and other assignments as well as group projects.

In small classes or within small groups in large classes, ask students to prepare their papers a few days early and provide copies prior to the class so that they can be read before their due date. This encourages collaboration among students in the class as well as more fully preparing student papers for a grade.

Students need to know each other if they are to develop a community for learning. In between class meetings, students can be encouraged to interact around class concepts through the use of class listservs and chat rooms. This interaction can involve posing questions that require students to respond using things learned in class, small group discussions of readings, or having students respond to one another's writing.

How to Incorporate Cooperative Learning

There are many ways to bring cooperative learning into the class and many approaches that apply across disciplines. (For a discussion of cooperative learning and a collection of activities, see Stein, 2000.) Several strategies provide a good foundation.

- Explain strategies for forming study groups.

- Encourage students to share papers in advance.

- Set up listservs or other online mechanisms (e.g., chat rooms) for students to meet between classes.

As classes get bigger on many college campuses—a major stress for new faculty—the above strategies can help to make classrooms within classrooms and to create community. The scenario below illustrates how a chair who promotes effective teaching may respond to a faculty member whose first year of teaching did not go as well as expected.

Scenario: A second-year faculty member had trouble with teaching a large class in her first year and is now faced with teaching the same course again. The chair saw the evaluations from year one, which were not very favorable, and talked to Eva about the class.

Response: The chair meets with the faculty member to discuss ideas for teaching large lecture classes and to offer available resources both on campus and in the literature. The chair also recommends she observe faculty on campus who have successfully taught large introductory sections of courses. The key to success for large classes is to make them not feel so large for students.

Most new faculty come to their positions with limited teaching experience. While some faculty are natural teachers and the talent to teach seems inborn, most instructors need to work on their teaching. Campuses that have teaching centers do well to target new faculty members and offer workshops on particular areas for development (e.g., preparing lectures, promoting active learning, dealing with large courses). Data from our research indicate that new faculty use teaching centers and benefit from their services. On campuses where there is the absence of an instructional development center, department chairs need to take a more active stance at the departmental level in developing effective teaching practices. In the following paragraphs, we provide a list of problems frequently encountered by new faculty and some ideas for department chairs to share with their faculty that can help promote effective teaching.

TEACHING PROBLEMS FREQUENTLY ENCOUNTERED BY JUNIOR FACULTY

The following is a list of teaching problems typically faced by junior faculty.

- Lack of expertise in subject matter
- Over-preparation of materials
- Over-reliance on lecture methods to the exclusion of interaction with students in the course
- Teaching above or below levels of students in the course
- Lack of coherence between course objectives and material presented
- Inundating students with too much information
- Lack of organization of materials for course time
- Lack of attention to the physical space of the classroom (e.g., lights, arrangement of chairs)
- Reluctance to ask for help with teaching
- Lack of awareness of how a course is going prior to end of course evaluations

To overcome these obstacles to effective teaching, we offer several suggestions for department chairs to share with their new faculty members. While many of these suggestions are geared to helping faculty with problems in large courses, these strategies can help faculty be effective teachers regardless of class content or size.

ADDRESSING PROBLEMS IN THE CLASSROOM

I taught the same rotation of courses the first two years I was here. Each semester I taught three courses—two sections of the same introductory course and one section of a senior seminar. This year I am teaching the introductory course, the senior seminar, and a required class for new majors. Overall, things are going quite well, but sometimes when I look out at the sea

*of faces in my classrooms, I have very little sense of how well
I'm doing. Do students get it? Am I teaching them the material they need? Do my methods of teaching reach students?*

Introductory courses, in particular, call upon faculty to be able to cover
materials in areas that may be outside of the faculty member's expertise.
Faculty can address this problem by reading about topics outside of their
specialty area and anticipating questions. Consult faculty with experience
teaching introductory courses to review their course materials and assignments. Chairs can help by consulting with new faculty about their preferences for courses to teach in the first year. While it may not always be possible to give them all the courses they want, talking to new faculty about
their strengths and weaknesses in the courses to be taught can help them
feel better about course assignments and can help you as a chair learn
about their specialties and areas of expertise.

Effective teachers, especially those of large classes, can be a great
resource for new teachers. New faculty can gain a lot from meeting with an
experienced teacher to go over their teaching philosophy, ways of preparation, and mechanisms for interaction with students, and then follow that
up with an observation of the course. Most faculty teach as they were
taught, so the more people that they observe teaching, the more likely they
are to gather essential information to help them develop as teachers.

Faculty need to think about what can reasonably be accomplished in a
particular semester and within a specified time in class. Preparation for
each class period should take into account the objectives for that session
and be made clear to students in the class. Chairs can assure that objectives
are reasonable by ascertaining that new faculty understand how the academic calendar works at the new institution and by sharing sample objectives from tried courses. New faculty might also benefit from guidance on
how to construct syllabi that will both fit into the semester and will incorporate various teaching and learning strategies. (For a good, brief source,
see Grunert, 1997.)

Although objectives should be part of all session plans, no one method
exists for organizing notes for class sessions. Possibilities include an outline
that provides an overview and general discussion points, note cards with
notes for material and ideas for presenting material, and diagrams that
map out ways to present material that include tangents, examples, and suggestions for involving students. Some new faculty may also use PowerPoint
presentations routinely in class. Faculty development sessions should stress

that the preparation for the course is more important than the notes the professor makes; however, offering new faculty sample lecture notes or lesson plans can be helpful.

The above suggestions are proactive ways in which new faculty can improve their teaching. However, problems may arise as the semester proceeds. Teaching problems can emanate from a lack of awareness about who students in the classroom are and what their level of preparation is for the course. Faculty can learn more about their students by having students submit information sheets at the beginning of the semester and by talking to colleagues and the department chair about the level of preparation students have for particular courses. Course materials can then be adapted to meet the needs of students. Listservs and informal meetings with students are additional ways to learn how students are responding to what is happening in the classroom.

Another way to assess students' knowledge and feelings about the course involves continual assessment. Too often faculty do not realize they are having trouble with a course until the course is over. It is useful to conduct formal midsemester and final evaluations to gauge progress and to make any necessary changes. Other evaluation strategies that can be used throughout the course include one-minute papers where students take a minute at the end of class to go over what they learned that day. This strategy can help the instructor determine if there is coherence between class objectives and student learning. Another strategy is the muddiest point paper where students articulate what is least clear to them about a particular topic or about the class in general. Midsemester evaluations will help faculty direct topics for subsequent class meetings to meet student needs more directly. Final course evaluations may be familiar to new faculty from graduate school teaching assistantship experiences, but many new faculty will not have been introduced to the idea of midsemester evaluations. Chairs interested in improving departmental teaching should consider introducing this practice to their faculty.

Scenario: Brian, a third-year faculty member has come to you about concerns he has with his teaching. He taught the same courses for his first two years, and now he has added a new course. Brian is feeling a little overwhelmed with all he has to do and is uncertain about his effectiveness as an instructor because his evaluations continue to be mediocre although he feels that his courses go well. Students rarely complain to him.

Response: Suggest to Brian that he do one-minute papers to assess students' progress throughout the semester. Help him become more self-aware about his teaching methodologies by going over a sample lesson plan. Encourage him to seek help from the faculty development office.

COMMON PRACTICES OF GOOD TEACHERS

In order for new faculty to become effective teachers, department chairs should encourage them to develop the following practices.

- Be comfortable with course material.

- Observe faculty who have successfully taught courses in problem areas.

- Set clear objectives for the course overall and for each class period.

- Develop a system for course notes that offers a guide, but is not so rigid as to disallow examples, explanations, class participation, and meaningful tangents.

- Get to know your students.

- Conduct evaluations throughout the semester.

Classroom Observations

> *I've kept all my syllabi. In three years, a handful of students have written notes saying they liked my class, and I've kept them in a file folder. A faculty member from another department lectured in my class and told me afterward he thought the class was well prepared. I asked him to write a note about it. I know it sounds hokey, but I was told to do it.*

Although the department chair may play a significant role in helping new faculty become good teachers, faculty development is not just a matter to be addressed by the department chair. Functional departments involve all faculty in the development of new colleagues. Just as faculty can benefit from sharing drafts of their written work with colleagues as a means to develop as researchers, so too can new faculty benefit from input from colleagues about teaching. One mechanism to solicit this input is through classroom observations.

Some departments make classroom observations a part of promotion and tenure evaluation. While such observation can be helpful, it can also be stressful for junior faculty members since they are officially being evaluated. From a development perspective, it may be more helpful for department chairs to make classroom observation available by invitation before any formal evaluations are done for the promotion and tenure process. One way this can work is to identify senior faculty who are effective in the classroom and then ask them if they are willing to observe and provide feedback to junior faculty. Junior faculty should then be informed of the faculty who are willing to observe and be encouraged to invite these faculty into the classroom. The purpose of these observations is to give constructive feedback and to provide the new faculty member with one more mechanism to improve their instruction. The following scenario illustrates one way in which observations may be used.

Scenario: Margaret's course evaluations are consistently average, which will not look good to the tenure committee. Students rarely rate her above a 3 on a 5-point scale, but she has no idea what she can do to raise her evaluations and improve her teaching.

Response: Match experienced faculty members who are proven in the classroom to observe newer faculty in their classes. This should not be done as part of an evaluation, but instead as a means to help the new faculty member assess how well they are doing in the classroom and to learn areas on which to focus for improvement.

Department chairs looking to this option as a way to create a culture of teaching by involving both senior and junior faculty, and as a means to help new faculty develop as teachers, should consider the following guidelines to arrange classroom observations:

- Observations should be by invitation only. Surprise visits are needlessly stressful.

- Senior faculty conducting the observations should be genuinely concerned with teaching improvement, not just with providing evaluation.

- Observations should be accompanied by written feedback that includes what the faculty member observed as done particularly well, what needs work, and suggestions for improvements.

- Observations should be followed up with a discussion with the junior faculty member as a means to put closure on the process.

- Observations should be done as a mechanism of development, not as a means of evaluation. In departments where classroom evaluation is part of formal evaluations there should also be opportunity for more informal evaluation that is focused on improvement.

Classroom Evaluations: Teaching and Tenure

While classroom evaluations can be useful tools for improving instruction, the weight these evaluations are given at tenure time may put additional stress on new faculty members. New faculty especially require help in interpreting and responding to course evaluations. A faculty member from a small liberal arts campus shared with us the following:

> *If you are talking about success as in getting tenure, I think the main item is that students need to be very positive about your abilities as a teacher. The teaching evaluation form is considered to be a primary yardstick at this school. They are more concerned with the students' written comments than with what the numbers are.*

In comparison, a faculty member from a doctoral-granting institution that values excellence in teaching and research shared her experience with teaching evaluations:

> *In my department it is expected that you will be at least a 4 on a five-point scale when it comes to teaching evaluations. From what I hear, anything below a 4 is considered really bad and is generally not acceptable in the annual review. Of course, teaching evaluations tend to be inflated, but the department is still really fixed on the numbers.*

Most administrators and promotion and tenure committees use the results of institutional evaluations to measure teaching effectiveness and performance for the promotion and tenure review process. Department chairs need to communicate to junior faculty how evaluations will be used in promotion and tenure. Are evaluations a central part of the review process? Is there attention given to both numeric and written information? Can faculty submit other materials to illustrate their teaching effectiveness? How will evaluations be used in the review process? The importance of answering such questions can be understood in the scenario given below.

Scenario: At the end of each semester, Hester gives her students the standard college evaluation forms. The results are tallied and given to faculty members a month into the following semester. Hester glances at her evaluations and then shoves them into a drawer to peruse when she has time. Her evaluations are consistently lower than other junior faculty. But with new courses to prepare for and several research projects to start, continue, or complete, she never gets around to reviewing these sheets. As a consequence, she never changes her teaching style because she does not know that anything needs to be improved.

Response: Chairs can encourage new faculty to use their own system of evaluation to elicit feedback from students while classes are in progress and to change strategies, if necessary, to better meet the learning needs of the students and ultimately to bolster end-of-semester evaluations.

What should a chair do if faced with a faculty member in a situation like the above? New faculty may blame low scores on the student evaluation instrument, making it essential that chairs "coach" new faculty on how to interpret the evaluation scores so that they can act on their shortcomings. Standardized evaluations are a tool department chairs can use to assess how junior faculty are doing with their teaching, but they are not flawless. Chairs need to consider multiple modes of assessment and encourage their faculty to conduct evaluations throughout the semester, use opportunities for classroom evaluations, and consider developing teaching portfolios.

PORTFOLIOS

Portfolios can be used both informally and formally. Many colleges and universities are moving toward portfolio-based assessment whereby faculty establish teaching goals for a semester or year and then use a portfolio to describe how these goals were reached. Portfolios as a mechanism for evaluation allow faculty members to assess their teaching effectiveness using multiple means. Consequently, portfolios are also useful for department chairs to see how the new faculty member is developing as an instructor. As indicated by Dr. Weimer in Chapter 9, relying solely on standardized evaluations to assess teaching is not very useful as a developmental tool. Portfolios, in contrast, can be used both formatively and summatively as a means to identify issues in the classroom that need to be addressed and to assess overall effectiveness. (See Seldin, 1997, for a good source on the preparation and use of portfolios.)

TEACHING SEMINARS

Teaching seminars are another way that department chairs can help new faculty as teachers. For example, at Hamline University, curriculum seminars have been used to develop faculty as specialists in their fields into educators. The seminars are centered around teaching and help faculty identify problems in their classroom and ways to remediate them. The main purpose of the seminars is to talk about teaching and learning and to help faculty meet their own personal goals for teaching in addition to the university's. Sessions tend to be informal and are focused on improvement and development as teachers and not just solely on evaluation.

Teaching Diverse Students

My evaluations were terrible. I wasn't structuring the material, and the students didn't know what to expect. At my previous institution, evaluations weren't required. I was quite surprised that students didn't come and talk to me because I don't consider myself intimidating or remote. I didn't discuss my poor evaluations with the seminar group since it didn't seem relevant. Mainly, I had problems between different age students in my classes, where the older, nontraditional ones and the young ones fresh out of college, seemed to rub each other the wrong way.

Students are changing in ways that require resources and expertise that are not always available on campus. Today's students are more challenging to teach, and faculty are often ill-equipped to respond to their diverse learning needs. In the past, faculty could rely on a fairly well-prepared cohort of 18- to 22-year-old students in their classroom. On many campuses today, these students are in the minority, yet there is still a tendency to teach to these students. Faculty, with support of their chairs, need to consider that the number one growing group of students is adults returning to school. Many of these nontraditional students have been in the workforce, and many are also experienced in college. Clearly, as illustrated in the above excerpt, their needs in the classroom are different than 18-year-olds in their first college class.

Chairs can help their faculty deal with diversity in the classroom by acquainting them with the research on student retention and how their interactions with students can contribute to increased student success. Most faculty are not aware of the voluminous literature on the impact of academic and social integration on student retention (see Tinto, 1987; Pascarella & Terenzini, 1991). For example, it has been fairly well established that students who interact with faculty outside of class (e.g., by seeking advice during office hours or stopping to chat about a topic) will be more engaged with their learning and feel more connected to their institutions, and hence, more committed to staying in school. It is also fairly well established that the students most likely to have the tools to achieve this sense of engagement are those who have been socialized—in the home and high schools—to being college students. Students from poor homes, from minority backgrounds, and also women, are the least likely to have the self-assurance to initiate such relationships. Faculty, particularly in undergraduate teaching-oriented institutions, need to be approachable and convey this clearly to their students.

Faculty can benefit from reading *Lives on the Boundary* (1989) in which Mike Rose narrates his experiences as a teacher of underprepared students at UCLA. Through accounts of his students' experiences and frustrations as they attempt to manage an alienating environment, Rose shows that professors who connect with their students on a personal level are more likely to create opportunities to learn for underprepared students. The number of college students who need remedial courses in basic skills continues to grow, and with it the requirement for faculty who have the versatility and knowledge to do more than simply "deposit" knowledge into students' heads.

The suggestions we provide for chairs to help their faculty improve instruction are to benefit not only junior faculty, but all faculty. Chairs who help develop new faculty as teachers are developing a departmental culture that values teaching. By involving all faculty in a push toward teaching effectiveness, the whole department is sure to improve as teachers.

FACULTY AS ADVISORS

An often overlooked component of the teaching role of new professors is advising. Most faculty have some type of advising responsibilities and, as with teaching, there is rarely any orientation or training on how to advise students. New faculty are typically assigned advisees, given a student handbook, and then meet with students to plan their coursework. Although most campuses have offices that specialize in cooperative education and career services, advising can also include giving advice on career options, internships, and graduate school. For the faculty member new to the profession, these responsibilities can be overwhelming. Department chairs can be useful to faculty in this regard by providing direction about productive advising.

According to research and experience by Richard J. Light (1992), advisors can help students make key decisions that will shape their entire college experience. Young men and women arriving at college immediately confront, and for most for the first time, serious life decisions: which courses to choose? what subject to specialize in? what major to choose? what activities to join? how much to study? how to study?

Such decisions are intensely personal. Often they are made with little information. Yet the consequences can be enormous. Advisors can play a crucial role in helping students negotiate these decisions. They can ask questions and make suggestions that have the potential to affect students profoundly. Typically, the advising relationship is ongoing throughout the college experience and is thus important to "get right" from the start.

Light's broad and overarching finding is that students' academic performance and satisfaction at college are tied closely to involvement with faculty and other students around substantive work. Why is college fulfilling for certain students and less so for others? Students report that certain course choices, decisions they make, and study habits lead to a successful college experience. Further, success in college is tied to making significant connections with professors both in and out of class. For many students, this connection is particularly important when it is with an advisor.

Academic involvement and academic success require interpersonal engagement. Nearly every student who describes strong academic performance can point to a specific activity that ties academic work closely to another person or a group of people. The other person is often a professor who is supervising the student's work in a small class or as a research assistant in work outside of class, and in many cases, the professor is the student's academic advisor. All of these roles require the professor to be acquainted with what works to develop a constructive advising relationship with students. A checklist at the end of this chapter provides information concerning what new faculty need to know about general student advising.

In a research university in particular, faculty are typically aware of the need to do exemplary research, but the role of teaching is often less certain. Good research does not always translate into good teaching. Institutional and department priorities with regard to teaching vary greatly. For example, the primary function of faculty at a liberal arts college may be teaching six or more courses a year. In comparison, faculty at research universities and some comprehensive universities may need to balance teaching as one of many requirements for tenure. In any case, the department chair's role in supporting good teaching is instrumental to the new faculty's future.

CHECKLIST: ADVISING (FOR FACULTY MEMBERS)

☐ Encourage students, and especially freshmen, to enroll in several small classes that encourage in-class interactions. This enables students to engage with others, to learn how to speak up, and to explore their interests more in depth.

☐ Recommend that students join study groups, especially for large courses. Study groups can help promote interpersonal involvement and provide community within the classroom. Encourage students to share papers in advance with both their instructors and their peers—perhaps in the writing center. Writing is a great source of stress for students, and the sooner students make writing a shared experience the sooner they can focus on developing as writers. Most students want to develop as writers but are unsure of how to do so. Too often, students hand in drafts of writing and then are discouraged by negative feedback. Engaging in writing as a process is a way to enhance written communication, research papers, and other written class assignments.

☐ Remind students that you are their advisor, but that meeting their requirements is their responsibility, so encourage them to ask questions, to plan their semester work in advance, and to read their catalogs and handbooks.

REFERENCES

Davis, B. G. (1993). *Tools for teaching.* San Francisco, CA: Jossey-Bass.

Education Commission of the States (ECS). (1996). What research says about improving undergraduate education: Twelve attributes of good practice. *AAHE Bulletin, 48* (8), 5-8.

Grunert, J. (1997). *The course syllabus: A learning-centered approach.* Bolton, MA: Anker.

Light, R. J. (1992). *The Harvard assessment seminars, second report: Explorations with students and faculty about teaching, learning, and student life.* Cambridge, MA: Harvard University, Graduate School of Education and Kennedy School of Government.

Pascarella, E., & Terenzini, P. (1991). *How college affects students.* San Francisco, CA: Jossey-Bass.

Rose, M. (1989). *Lives on the boundary.* New York, NY: Penguin Books.

Seldin, P. (1997). *The teaching portfolio: A practical guide to improved performance and promotion/tenure decisions* (2nd ed.). Bolton, MA: Anker.

Stein, R. F. (2000). *Cooperative learning: A faculty guide to teamwork in the classroom.* Bolton, MA: Anker.

Tinto, V. (1987). *Leaving college: Rethinking the causes and cures of student attrition.* Chicago, IL: University of Chicago Press.

CHAPTER 14

MONITORING SERVICE OBLIGATIONS

Almost 50% of my time is spent on committees. The problem is that we don't have enough senior faculty to go around, and those who are senior don't want to serve. The department chair feels he doesn't have a choice, and the dean seems oblivious. There are always good reasons to put me on a committee; it's just that I don't think it will help me get tenure.

The problem with committee work is that it's busy work. It takes time, so I avoid it, and in general the department chair tries to shield me from it, too.

These two responses illustrate the central role department chairs can play in helping junior faculty with service obligations. The first respondent knows that all of his committee work will cut into time for teaching and research, but because his department chair does not help him protect his time, there is little he can do to cut down on these responsibilities. The second faculty member—because she is fortunate enough to have the support of her department chair—has not been bogged down with too many committee responsibilities.

Although all institutions require some kind of service of their faculty, none of them value service work a great deal when it comes time for the tenure and promotion process. The role service plays in promotion and tenure decisions varies by institutional type, but little information about the importance (or unimportance) of service is communicated directly to junior faculty. However, in working with junior faculty, the department chair must articulate how service works on that campus. Department chairs can easily tell faculty they need to engage in professional (i.e., national conference activities, editorial boards) and public (i.e., campus committee work) service, but letting faculty know how much service is enough is a more difficult task.

GUIDING SERVICE CHOICES

I haven't published very much, but my service is the best in the college, and my teaching is good. I think they'll take that into account. (Tierney & Bensimon, 1996, p. 69)

My department chair told me I should get on college-wide committees because that's the way faculty in the other departments get to know you. (Tierney & Bensimon, 1996, p. 69)

Department Chair: *It's not a good idea for younger people to stay hidden away. I see it as my responsibility to put them on committees where they learn about the institution, and the rest of us learn about them.* (Tierney & Bensimon, 1996, p. 69)

Chair of Promotion and Tenure Committee: *Service is hard to evaluate when we go over someone's files, but it's also the only time, probably, that somebody in another department has had to meet the person or know what he's done. "Oh, he served on that task force last year. That was a bear," someone will say, and they'll think well of the candidate for it.* (Tierney & Bensimon, 1996, p. 69)

Chairs can help junior faculty select which service appointments will best serve their needs and those of the institution. While service is often considered to be rather onerous, serving on committees can be good opportunities for internal networking and meeting colleagues from other departments and divisions. The chairs in the excerpts above recognize the positive aspects of service and can communicate how service works on their campuses.

Junior faculty often find it difficult to know what service assignments to accept and what ones to turn down. This problem is exacerbated by service duties that are difficult to monitor, such as working with students. Popular teachers and people who represent a minority—racial, gender, sexual orientation—are often inundated with students who need help, advice, or a willing ear. While these duties can be very important, the department chair needs to help these faculty guard their time and energy so that they do not place service as a top priority in place of teaching and research. The following scenario illustrates how committee work may interfere with other academic obligations.

Scenario: Neal, an outgoing assistant professor, finds himself on several committees both within his own department and as departmental representative for university-wide committees. He spends so much time on his service work that his teaching preparation comes second, and his research projects have been shoved back to a distant third. He finds it easier to meet commitments that he knows are coming up next week or next month than worrying about tenure, which is four years away.

Response: Make known the relative role that service plays in the tenure review process, and monitor the junior faculty's service activities in twice-yearly meetings to ensure an appropriate balance. If necessary, negotiate service loads with deans and university representatives. Remember that a strict accounting of the number of service obligations is not all the information you may need in order to monitor these activities. Some committees, for example, require much more work, time, and attention than others.

What can department chairs do to help faculty like Neal who want to be contributing university citizens and help students while maintaining a productive research agenda? The key to success with the tenure process is balance. Faculty first need to learn the expectations for tenure, and then they must balance those expectations accordingly. The role of service, depending on the institution, can range from negligible to central in importance for tenure decisions. The chair can help new faculty properly navigate service responsibilities.

Although some kind of service is inevitable for junior faculty, choosing service obligations that will have some positive impact on their careers can compensate for what may be routine and often time-consuming work. Positive choices may include committees chaired by powerful faculty in the institution, task forces likely to catch the attention and approbation of the dean, or service projects close to the faculty member's past experience or research interests.

In addition to which particular service responsibilities junior faculty take on, the chair should also help new faculty weigh the volume of responsibilities. Is there an institutional "formula" for how much service is required? For example, at one of our research sites, faculty are required to sit on two department committees (one of which they must chair), one college committee, and one university-wide committee. If faculty meet these service expectations by the time they come up for promotion and tenure review, then their service contributions should be deemed adequate by the promotion and tenure committee. If the department chair offers firm ideas about how much service is adequate for success, then faculty are at an advantage in creating balance in their professional lives.

While all junior faculty are likely to be unprepared for the amount of service expected of them, some segments of the faculty population are overwhelmed with service requests because of who they are. Women and people of color are sometimes called upon to serve on campus, college, or department committees as representatives of their gender and/or race, so they often become overburdened with service responsibilities. One of our respondents discusses this problem:

> *Service counts for only 20% of the evaluation, and I do three to four times as much as any faculty person. . . . [Because] I am Latino, I get a fairly substantial trickle of minority students who come here, not necessarily to be advised in the traditional, more formal sort of way, but just to come by to talk and explore their problems, to tell me that they can't handle this institution any more because it is so white. Or, to let me know that a situation at home is intolerable . . . so I have that kind of double role to play in terms of academic, but also more of a personal advisor role, and that takes up a lot of my time. The institution does not recognize that minority faculty have an extra load by being minorities. . . . I enjoy doing it, but it needs to be rewarded.*
> (Tierney & Bensimon, 1996, p. 115)

While it is important for committees to have the representation of women and people of color, chairs should make sure that tenure-track faculty are not overloaded with service responsibilities. The following scenario outlines how easily junior faculty can become involved in too much service.

Scenario: Amy is in her second tenure-track position. She came to State University after an unfavorable fourth-year review at Research

University. In spite of favorable teaching evaluations, involvement in university and disciplinary service, and what was considered by her departmental peers as "average" research productivity, Amy was told she was not "tenureable material" at Research University. She has just completed her first year at State and, as she puts it, "is simply overloaded with student advising and committee work." Amy is the only African American and the only woman in the department, and in her estimation, the only faculty member who cares about students and wants to be involved in the life of the university.

Response: The department chair should monitor faculty involvement in service activities, encourage faculty to say "no" to an onerous level of involvement in service, and support their decisions not to serve. Special care needs to be given to faculty overburdened with hidden service responsibilities.

Faculty are expected to share a commitment to university governance and service. As long as the numbers of women and people of color in faculty positions remain low, they will disproportionately be called upon to fill service posts. At the department level, the chair is in a position to monitor the level of faculty service involvement and assure equity in assignments. At the college and university levels, chairs may have more difficulty protecting faculty from becoming overburdened with service responsibilities.

Department chairs need to be advocates for new faculty and to negotiate with the dean and other senior level administrators to keep the service commitments of faculty manageable, particularly for women and people of color. Although shared responsibility for university governance is important, and service is fundamental to the maintenance of any college, university, or discipline, service should not overshadow other important aspects of a junior faculty member's first few years. With the movement toward more inclusive and culturally diverse campus communities, chairs need to assure that service assignments are equitably distributed and give faculty a realistic appraisal of the reward for service involvement relative to other requirements for promotion and tenure.

CHECKLIST: MONITORING SERVICE OBLIGATIONS

☐ Don't ask new faculty to serve on time-consuming committees nor to serve as chairs of committees.

☐ Assign new faculty to service activities that will help them gain a better understanding of the department or institution and will facilitate their integration.

☐ Help new faculty make wise choices for service responsibilities.

☐ Make service expectations clear for the promotion and tenure process, and provide opportunities to fulfill them.

☐ Help faculty learn to say "no" to service requests.

☐ Negotiate service loads at the college and university level.

REFERENCE

Tierney, W. G., & Bensimon, E. M. (1996). *Promotion and tenure: Community and socialization in academe.* Albany, NY: SUNY Press.

⊸ CHAPTER 15 ⊸

EXPLAINING EVALUATION PROCEDURES

At my third-year review, I was told I had to boost the quality of my publications. The college-wide committee was concerned that my publications weren't substantive and theoretically focused. I met with my chair to come up with strategies on dealing with the committee's concerns and to develop a focused line of inquiry. I worked tirelessly in my fourth year to get additional publications and I also got a fairly large external grant. I feel pretty good about all that I've accomplished. We'll see what the committee thinks come promotion and tenure time.

In year one the chair told me to work on teaching, so I did. In year two my chair didn't think I had enough publications, so I boosted my publications. At my third-year review, my contract was not renewed because of problems with my teaching. I'm still not exactly sure what the problems were with my teaching, but I'm tired of dealing with moving targets. It's not worth the battle.

In this chapter we discuss the chair's ongoing role in guiding assistant professors in the specifics of evaluation for promotion and tenure to help them avoid the problems experienced by the two assistant professors above. This chapter includes recommendations for the development of informational materials as well as how to conduct annual and mid-probationary reviews and develop a list of external reviewers.

Department chairs need to be proactive about preparing information on promotion and tenure and reviewing it with assistant professors on a regular basis. Assistant professors need guidance to understand who to talk to and what questions to ask; the process should be initiated by the department chair and senior faculty in the department. A systematic process will assure that all new faculty are treated equitably. Some faculty are naturally able to socialize with others and find out the unspoken rules; however, there are also many who will not feel comfortable in initiating such conversations or who will be unsuccessful in breaking into departmental cliques (Tierney & Bensimon, 1996). For example, an African-American professor going up for tenure told us that the kind of help he got from the faculty in the Ethnic Studies Department would never have been offered by the senior faculty in his department unless he was the one to initiate the request for help. He said, "You always feel comfortable approaching people there [in the Ethnic Studies Department], and when you talk to people you know they are interested in you. There is an eagerness to share documents such as a tenure file, what a tenured person did, how it went" (Tierney & Bensimon, 1996, pp. 110-111). When the time came for putting together his application for tenure this same faculty member said, "They showed me how to put the personal statement together . . . one of my colleagues spent three hours with me, and we went through everything" (p. 111). The lesson to be learned from this example is that the chair should not assume that a lack of questions from a new faculty member signals that all is well. Similarly, rather than simply telling new faculty to network, it is more valuable to describe ways in which networking can be dovetailed into one's regular schedule to make it part of the job.

If part of networking at your institution involves cultivating names of potential external reviewers, then it is important to inform new faculty of the ways in which the new professor can become known to others. Earlier we discussed service obligations as a way to network. The chair may also recommend that the junior faculty member share papers with a list of respected peers in other institutions. Having such a list available helps the new faculty member develop as a scholar and become known to potential reviewers. Another strategy is to encourage new faculty to attend conferences and present papers and panels that bring together experienced scholars and newcomers. What new faculty need to understand is that they have to make themselves known to others, and the best way of doing so is by establishing connections based on mutual academic and teaching interests.

To help junior faculty cultivate networks, we advise chairs to develop a promotion and tenure handbook that offers individuals the information they will need to put together their promotion and tenure dossier. This handbook should also include sample documents that reflect the institution's required format for the promotion and tenure dossier. It should also alert the assistant professor to what they should avoid doing. The handbook should describe the criteria used to determine teaching performance, research performance, and service performance. It should also include the sequence of events for the promotion and tenure process and give specific dates for the completion of each stage of the process, including the date by which candidates should expect to hear the outcome. It is also important to describe how the outcome is communicated to the candidate (e.g., a confidential letter, a personal meeting). Other useful information to include in the handbook are the conditions under which it is possible to petition for early tenure decision and circumstances that permit stopping the tenure clock (e.g., childbirth).

We also suggest that chairs hold an annual review meeting with assistant professors. The purpose of the meeting should be to review their progress, make adjustments as needed in workload, and discuss what each individual will need to have in his or her files by the tenure review time. For example, if the institution requires that the file include a specified number of letters from senior faculty attesting to the candidate's teaching effectiveness, make sure the candidate is aware of the requirement and help him or her identify who should do the observations and when they should take place. As part of this review, alert the candidate to the need for collecting names of individuals who might serve as external reviewers of the candidate's work. Reviewers should be from a national pool and be familiar with the content of the candidate's work. Annual meetings provide a good opportunity for the chair to coach the newcomer on what their focus should be for the final review. Ask the assistant professor to do some of the following tasks.

- Describe their research agenda (e.g., the theoretical underpinnings, the larger body of research that informs it, new understandings the research is producing, and so on).

- Provide the names of individuals in other institutions who are familiar with their work and could serve as external reviewers.

- Describe specific ways in which they have improved their teaching or introduced innovations in the classroom.

The purpose of asking the assistant professor to articulate these areas is to alert him or her to the practicalities of the review process. If in the second or third year on the tenure track, the newcomer is not able to describe his or her research agenda in a manner that reflects a unified focus or is unable to come up with names of individuals who know his or her work and could serve as external reviewers, the chair will know that this professor is in need of serious coaching.

Annual meetings also provide an opportunity for the chair to learn whether the newcomer is taking advantage of institution-based grant opportunities for research and professional development. For example, Santa Clara University has a junior faculty fellowship program that is designed to provide young scholars with an extended period of time for full-time research and sufficient funds to cover the basic costs of the research project. Recipients of the fellowship continue to receive full salary while being released from all teaching and other university assignments and $3,500 to cover project expenses. New faculty may be aware that these grants exist but may not apply because they don't think they will receive them or because they don't know how to write a grant application. Chairs can help new faculty overcome this hurdle by freely sharing examples of winning grant applications and by offering to read first drafts and provide comments. Annual meetings should always be followed up with a letter that is supportive but provides a candid assessment of the newcomer's strengths and weaknesses as well as concrete recommendations for actions to be taken.

Arrange for the dean to meet with assistant professors at least once a year. The dean will have a more global view than the department chair or candidate about the requirements and changes in institutional goals that could impact the promotion and tenure review. It is also important for the dean to be familiar with the candidate's work, as the dean will be the one to make the final recommendation on whether to support the candidate for promotion and tenure.

In addition to these one-on-one meetings, chairs interested in monitoring the progress of their junior faculty can devise faculty development opportunities that support the process of preparing for tenure review. One suggestion is to provide each new faculty member with a copy of Robert Diamond's (1995) *Preparing for Promotion and Tenure Review: A Faculty Guide,* and to conduct one or two orientation sessions about the ongoing nature of building a dossier for review.

Preparing for the Mid-Probationary Review

Campuses vary on how they conduct their reviews. While some review faculty on an annual basis, most conduct some type of mid-probationary review (e.g., in the third year). The purpose of such a review is variable, but it is vital to make the purpose clear and to enunciate possible outcomes. Junior faculty deserve to know whether the review is purely a formality or whether it can result in a decision to terminate. Candidates should also know whether the mid-probationary report accompanies the promotion and tenure dossier. Finally, candidates must be informed that a positive mid-probationary review is not a guarantee of tenure.

Tenure-track faculty should have a comprehensive review of their work at the midpoint of their probationary status, around the third year. Even if campuses do annual reviews, this review should be conducted to let faculty know of their progress toward tenure. The size of the department will determine whether all faculty should participate in the review or whether a committee will be charged with the responsibility. The review process should conclude with a written report that summarizes the individual's strengths and weaknesses and provides concrete recommendations about what he or she should do during the remainder of the time on the tenure track in order to satisfy departmental and university or college expectations for tenure. When a faculty appears to have a weak case and is not likely to be reviewed positively for tenure, the department should consider recommending nonreappointment or counsel the individual to resign. Such action will give the candidate ample time to develop his or her dossier or to seek other employment opportunities. The mid-probationary letter should be both summative, making clear the candidate's progress to tenure, and formative, highlighting areas of concern that the candidate needs to address. A sample letter appears at the end of this chapter.

The Promotion and Tenure Dossier

All institutions have a set of directions to follow in assembling the dossier, and one of the critical roles played by the chair is making sure that the candidate faithfully follows these directions. Additionally, department secretaries who have been trained to format dossiers and are familiar with the do's and don'ts can make the process less stressful and time-consuming for the chair and the candidate.

Anxious candidates frequently assume that the more items in their dossier, the more likely they are to be viewed as hard-working and productive academics. Such is rarely the case, however, and overloading the dossier can backfire. If candidates include every single flyer related to presentations given on and off campus, they create the impression that they do not have sufficient evidence of substantive accomplishments. Diamond (1995) advises that the documentation in the dossier should stress two dimensions: 1) the quality of the work and (2) the significance of the work. Further, he suggests that "Faculty may provide promotion and tenure committees with detailed information as to the quality of their effort but neglect to present a case for the value of their work, describing its impact or explaining in what ways and for whom this work has significance" (p. 22). The chair's role is to coach the new professor in how to communicate the quality and significance of the work and to help the candidate assemble a focused and manageable dossier wherein materials selected represent the candidate's best accomplishments and work.

One of the most critical yet neglected aspects of the dossier is the candidate's essay explaining his/her accomplishments. Chairs need to explain the purposes of this essay and to provide guidelines for how it should be written, what should be included, and how long it should be. Candidates often have a tendency to make the essay too long. One of us just reviewed a dossier with a 19-page essay, and we were surprised that the chair had allowed it to go forward to the final stages of review. Promotion and tenure committees are likely to resent being asked to digest a 19-page essay. The excessive length may raise questions about why the candidate needs 19 pages of self-explanation. While the candidate can be faulted for naiveté, it is the chair who has shown bad judgment by neglecting to advise the candidate to cut the essay down to a more manageable size.

Diamond (1995) recommends that the essay provide information that is not obvious from the materials included in the dossier, such as the following:

- A rationale for the choices that the candidate made (e.g., regarding a research agenda, teaching strategies)

- The extent to which the candidate has met his or her expectations

- Circumstances that promoted or inhibited success (however, we caution against an extended jeremiad)

- The significance of the work as an intellectual contribution to the field

- A map for the committee detailing the organization of the materials being submitted

THE EXTERNAL REVIEW PROCESS

Campuses vary in their reliance upon external reviews as an additional means to evaluate tenure candidates for promotion. Where external reviewers are used, it is of utmost importance for candidates to submit a list of names of people to evaluate their work. The list is typically submitted by the faculty member, and then the chair of the department will solicit input. As we have mentioned throughout this handbook, developing networks is an important part of the tenure process. A benefit of junior faculty involvement with disciplinary networks is to meet the requirements for outside reviewers in the promotion and tenure process. At a conference we attended recently, we were surprised to hear a second-year, tenure-track faculty member say:

> *I'm not sure about the outside review process. I have heard it alluded to, but I have never spoken with my department chair about the tenure process so specifically.*

A more academically shrewd respondent to our research offered his plan for finding positive outside reviewers:

> *I'm cultivating names. I have been working on that since day one. When I complete an article, I send it to a list I have of ten to 15 people. I always send my work to them. People need to know you. If you haven't thought about the process, you don't see this. I also go to four conferences a year. I network. There's always more than one reason you do something; it takes time for people to know you, to know your work, and they have to know you. There's nothing worse than getting an outside letter than begins "I've never heard of this person."* (Tierney & Bensimon, 1996, p. 72)

These two people have approached the issue of outside reviewers in completely different ways. The first person is clearly bemused by the process and needs guidance in negotiating tricky political waters. The second person possesses the political savvy to complete the tenure track with little mentoring help. However, few junior faculty members are as cognizant of how to handle the process as this assistant professor; most need the guidance of their department chair.

As a research agenda is established, the chair should recommend a timeline for faculty to identify suitable reviewers. For faculty working in areas where colleagues do not have depth of knowledge to review the candidate's work substantively, and for women and people of color doing research in areas that are considered "nonmainstream," the outside reviewer becomes critical by validating the new scholarship of junior faculty. Nothing is more anxiety-producing or disadvantageous for faculty during the final evaluation than to have to find suitable senior scholars in the field at the last minute. Thinking about outside reviewers early in the process is also a way for new faculty to familiarize themselves and get comfortable with being evaluated. Additionally, the process of "going public" allows women and people of color to gain access to the inner circles of the discipline. To succeed in academia requires that all faculty regularly be judged by their peers.

HOW TO IDENTIFY APPROPRIATE EXTERNAL REVIEWERS

As new faculty begin the process of selecting external reviewers, the suggestions that follow will provide them with a basis upon which to begin their search.

- Select senior faculty in the field that are familiar with the candidate's research as it relates to the discipline.

- Look for faculty who are based in an academic setting.

- Do not select a person with whom the faculty member has collaborated (e.g., coauthors, prior mentors).

- Choose faculty from a similar type of institution to that of the candidate's.

- If the candidate is in a highly specialized area, solicit someone with the same theoretical orientation or methodological expertise.

THE CHAIR'S LETTER FOR TENURE AND PROMOTION

One of the most important responsibilities of the chair is to coordinate the tenure and promotion process. The letter that accompanies the dossier should evaluate the candidate's strengths and weaknesses and provide assessments of their teaching, scholarship or artistic work, and service. The letter should also directly address any aspects of the dossier that need clarification and make a clear recommendation for or against tenure.

If the dossier includes materials that support the candidate's effectiveness as a teacher, such as course syllabi, tests, assignments, or documentation of activities undertaken to improve teaching effectiveness, the chair's responsibility is to interpret these materials for the promotion and tenure committee. Without explanatory comment, such materials will do little to support the candidate's tenure; thus, the chair can help support the faculty member's candidacy by explaining how these materials evidence high quality in teaching.

In large institutions, the promotion and tenure committee is usually composed of individuals who will not be familiar with either the candidate's work or disciplinary field. In view of this, the candidate and the chair have to be very attentive to explaining the significance of certain activities. Someone outside of the field of education will not be able to differentiate between a presentation at the American Educational Research Association (AERA) and the American Association for Higher Education (AAHE). However, if the candidate is seeking tenure at an institution that puts a premium on research, being in the program of the former group is far more prestigious than the latter. In contrast, if the candidate's institution places emphasis on the connection between scholarship and practice, a presentation at the meeting of the second group may carry greater weight. Similarly, the dossier as well as the chair's letter should address the professional stature of the journals that have published the candidate's work. Publications in refereed journals should be separated from those appearing in nonrefereed journals. In the area of service, solely providing a list of the committees served on by the candidate is not very useful. Both the candidate and the chair should explain what the individual's membership on a particular committee or committees accomplished.

A chair who takes this responsibility seriously will write a letter that reassures members of the promotion and tenure committee that the chair and senior members of the department have put the candidate's dossier through rigorous academic scrutiny. Too often department chairs have fallen into the role of either apologist for the candidate or clerical staff in charge of getting the dossier to the proper offices on time. We suggest that the chair plays the most critical role as the interpreter and judge of the candidate's achievements against institution-wide criteria.

Our assumption is that if the candidate has reached the sixth year in the tenure track there must have been evidence that the candidate was meeting the institution's criteria for promotion and tenure; otherwise the candidate would not have been reappointed following the mid-probationary review. Obviously, not all assistant professors who reach the sixth year on the tenure track are promoted and tenured.

An important responsibility of the department chair is to ensure that all candidates are afforded the support and opportunities to be successful. At the same time, it is also the responsibility of the chair not to reappoint someone whose record is clearly below expectations. The chair's role is to advise candidates of what they need to do in order to produce a promotion and tenure dossier that meets the institution's requirements. Not all junior faculty will accept or act on the advice given by the chair. Some individuals will not heed the advice given to them (e.g., attend a workshop on teaching, share manuscripts with colleagues) or will be resentful when told to cut down on service activities that do not count, or to extend preparation for teaching.

It is not our expectation that chairs will be therapists and attempt to change individuals who persist in self-defeating behaviors. Our focus has been on how chairs, through their leadership, can create a climate for success for junior faculty who may not know the rules but are motivated to learn them when shown. With that in mind, we have conceived of this as a handbook on the basic strategies that will enable chairs to be proactive in the professional development of the department's future generation of senior faculty.

THE FINAL EVALUATION: PREPARATION AND POLITICS

Evaluation is central to the relationship between the department chair and tenure-track faculty, and good chairs constantly evaluate their faculty. The thrust of this book has been to guide chairs in assisting junior faculty to engage in scholarly work that will be recognized as meritorious, to become effective teachers, to be productive members of the department, and to prepare a dossier that gives evidence of these accomplishments for tenure review.

Tenure evaluations are filled with formalities, informalities, and politics. As a senior member of the department, the responsible department chair has knowledge of the tenure process at the departmental, college, and institutional level and fully informs junior faculty of relevant policies and political nuances. If this handbook has been well used, preparing the final dossier for tenure review will be a matter of filling in the blanks and compiling information according to institutionally specified formats. The content will already exist.

The promotion and tenure review process—whether the first, second, or final review—is also an opportunity for the faculty member to share her or his work with the larger university community. The department chair and faculty member who have worked together should be able to develop a package that offers comprehensive documentation of the faculty's accomplishments; this package can be presented to succeeding levels of decision-makers in a way that meets all requirements for a successful review.

It would be naive, however, to suggest that preparing a comprehensive dossier and accomplishing acclaimed teaching, research, and service activities will guarantee tenure. At times even the most well-prepared, qualified candidate will not succeed with the review process. Tenure is an inherently political process. Certain parts of the process cannot be demystified because institutional political contexts vary. The political aspects of the process can only be understood by faculty insiders who are part of the inner circle. We, like other outsiders, are not privy to the invisible machinations of the tenure process. This insider/outsider dichotomy is a salient factor in the lower rates of tenure for those who stand outside the inner circle, such as women and people of color. Not being participants in the tenure decision-making process will not serve them well. The political process can undermine the efforts of even the most prepared faculty member. Using this handbook, we believe, will help chairs clarify the process for junior faculty and ensure every chance to gain tenure.

Considering the resources expended to hire competent junior faculty, the interests of the institution are best served when the talent of new faculty is nurtured. Too often we hear from new faculty that the tenure process is a system of exclusion rather than inclusion. Granted, not every junior faculty member is qualified or interested in the award of tenure. Well-preparedness mitigates against the politics of the tenure review process and increases the chances for promotion and tenure.

CHECKLIST: PROVIDING CONTINUOUS SUPPORT FOR EVALUATION

☐ Develop a promotion and tenure handbook or guidelines.

☐ Hold annual review meetings with all untenured faculty.

☐ Support research and grant-writing activities.

☐ Alert candidates to the need for collecting names of individuals who might serve as external reviewers of their work.

☐ Arrange for the dean to meet annually with assistant professors.

☐ Promote faculty development activities that aid in successful progress.

Sample Mid-Probationary Review Letter

Dear Candidate:

The college guidelines on tenure and promotion mandate a mid-probationary review in which the tenured faculty of the department are expected to evaluate all aspects of the candidate's teaching, scholarship or artistic work, and service with the same thoroughness, as far as possible, as these are evaluated in a review for tenure. What follows is our formal assessment of your work.

Procedure

While this letter of assessment neither assures success nor predicts failure at tenure time, the recommendations given here should be accorded a high degree of importance since the department will refer to them in its final tenure review. In accordance with the university's guidelines for promotion and tenure, you have the opportunity to discuss this letter with the department chair and submit a response prior to its formal submission to the dean.

Teaching

Your teaching record excels in several respects. Despite large classes, your evaluations have consistently been very good. You have also shown exceptional flexibility and skill in addressing departmental curricula needs well beyond your academic specialty, most notably in your work on the "Introduction to Society and Religion" course and in your development of the course, "Religious Traditions in Minority Communities." We also note your consistent interest in course development, innovation, and experimentation. In particular, your participation in two AACU curriculum development projects, two faculty workshops, and a teaching grant for curriculum development testifies to a consistent and energetic commitment to the highest quality teaching. In addition, you have undertaken a significant role in advising.

In our judgment, your record shows clear progress toward fulfilling the criteria in the area of teaching for both advancement to tenure and promotion to associate professor.

Research

With regard to your scholarship, we have been impressed by your professional approach to research and publication even while carrying a heavy teaching load. You have published four articles or book chapters in the three years you have been here, most of them in highly rated refereed journals or in publication projects with top-level university presses.

Your active participation and leadership in national scholarly groups clearly demonstrates that you have earned the respect and confidence of your colleagues.

We also note that you have a book in progress and look forward to seeing the completion of the manuscript in the near future.

In our judgment, your record of research and publication demonstrate excellent progress toward fulfillment of the criteria in the area of research for both advancement to tenure and promotion to associate professor.

Service

With regard to service, your record goes well beyond the expectations of service for pretenured faculty and hence is not only exemplary but also exceptional. We particularly note your consistent involvement in both formal and informal projects to contribute to the intellectual life of the campus. Our only concern is that you do not let your service activities overwhelm your research plans, which have such potential for contribution to the university as well. In the area of collegiality, you have shown yourself a valuable and congenial member of the department and university community.

In our judgment, you demonstrate excellent progress toward fulfilling the criteria in the area of service for both advancement to tenure and promotion to associate professor.

Conclusion

It is our assessment that your full record demonstrates excellent progress and professional excellence in the areas necessary for tenure and promotion. We urge you to complete your book-length manuscript and move toward concrete plans for its publication by a good press. To facilitate such a large project, we would urge you to cut back significantly from such active service on campus until the book project is secure.

Sincerely,

Eric LaMarque, Chair and Professor

CHECKLIST: PROMOTION AND TENURE
(TO BE COMPLETED BY THE CANDIDATE'S DEPARTMENT CHAIR)

Does the dossier include

☐ candidate's essay?

☐ candidate's curriculum vitae?

☐ department head's recommendation?

☐ description of the position?

☐ justification of every piece of information included as evidence of fulfilling quality criteria for teaching, scholarship and research, and service?

☐ departmental and college (where applicable) criteria for promotion and tenure?

☐ department committee's recommendation?

Does the candidate's curriculum vitae show

☐ complete chronology of candidate's education and professional career to date?

☐ courses taught?

☐ all degrees received by candidate, with institutions identified?

☐ publications separated into books and monographs, chapters, refereed journal articles, abstracts, research reports, other?

☐ page lengths for publications?

☐ percent of responsibilities for each coauthored publication?

Letters of evaluation

☐ external letters of assessment and a copy of the letter requesting an assessment of the candidate as well as a brief description of the academic stature of the external referees?

☐ letters received from outside referees included?

Evidence of quality

☐ Did the candidate submit a summary of student evaluations?

☐ Did the candidate discuss the significance of his/her scholarly work in the essay? (e.g., how his or her publications add to the literature or why their textbooks are different from others on the same topic)

☐ Did the candidate submit copies of published work?

Chair's letter

☐ Does the letter provide a balanced discussion of scholarship, teaching, and service?

☐ Does the letter explain how the candidate's work contributes to the mission of the department and institution?

☐ Does the letter explain any areas of inconsistencies, particularly circumstances that affected the work of the candidate?

☐ Does the letter concentrate on evidence rather than generalities?

☐ Does the letter address issues raised by external reviewers?

☐ Does the letter address the future potential of the candidate?

REFERENCES

Diamond, R. M. (1995). *Preparing for promotion and tenure review: A faculty guide.* Bolton, MA: Anker.

Tierney, W. G., & Bensimon, E. M. (1996). *Promotion and tenure: Community and socialization in academe.* Albany, NY: SUNY Press.

BIBLIOGRAPHY

Arreola, R. A. (1995). *Developing a comprehensive faculty evaluation system.* Bolton, MA: Anker.

Baldwin, R. G. (1990). Faculty career stages and implications for professional development. In J. H. Schuster & D.W. Wheeler (Eds.), *Enhancing faculty careers: Strategies for development and renewal* (pp. 20-40). San Francisco, CA: Jossey-Bass.

Bakst, D. (1999). *Student privacy on campus.* Washington, DC: Council on Law in Higher Education.

Bednash, G. P. (1991). Tenure review: Process and outcomes. *Review of Higher Education, 15* (1), 47-63.

Bell, C., Brock, R., & Gildensoph, L. (1993). *Guide to the perplexing: An introductory survival manual for new College of Liberal Arts faculty at Hamline.* St. Paul, MN: Hamline University.

Bland, C. J., & Schmitz, C. (1986). Characteristics of the successful researcher: Implications for faculty development. *Journal of Medical Education, 61*(1).

Boice, R. (1992). *The new faculty member: Supporting and fostering professional development.* San Francisco, CA: Jossey-Bass.

Boice, R. (1996). *First-order principles for college teachers: Ten basic ways to improve the teaching process.* Bolton, MA: Anker.

Boice, R., & Jones, F. (1984). Why academicians don't write. *Journal of Higher Education, 55* (5), 567-582.

Boyer, E. L. (1990). *Scholarship reconsidered: Priorities of the professoriate.* Princeton, NJ: The Carnegie Foundation for the Advancement of Teaching.

Braskamp, L. A. (1994). *Annual review of faculty achievements and contributions.* Chicago, IL: University of Illinois, Chicago.

Braskamp, L. A., & Ory, J. C. (1994). *Assessing faculty work: Enhancing individual and institutional performance.* Thousand Oaks, CA: Sage.

Bukalski, P. J. (1993). *Guide for nontenured faculty members: Annual evaluation, promotion, and tenure.* Atlanta, GA: University Film and Video Association.

Centra, J. A. (1993). *Reflective faculty evaluation: Enhancing teaching and determining faculty effectiveness.* San Francisco, CA: Jossey-Bass.

Chait, R. (1998). *Ideas in incubation: Three possible modifications to traditional tenure procedures.* Washington, DC: AAHE.

Chesler, M. A., & Crowfoot, J. E. (1989). *Racism in higher education.* Ann Arbor, MI: University of Michigan.

Chickering, A. W., & Gamson, Z. F. (1991). *Applying the seven principles for good practice in undergraduate education.* San Francisco, CA: Jossey-Bass.

Chism, N. (1999). *Peer review of teaching: A sourcebook.* Bolton, MA: Anker.

Clark, S. M., & Corcoran, M. (1986). Perspectives on the professional socialization of women faculty: A case of accumulative disadvantage. *Journal of Higher Education, 57,* 20-43.

Coiner, C., & Hume, D. (1998). *The family track: Keeping your faculties while you mentor, nurture, teach, and serve.* Urbana, IL: University of Illinois Press.

Covey, S. R. (1995). *The seven habits of highly effective people: Powerful lessons in personal change.* Provo, UT: Covey Leadership Center.

Creswell, J. W., & Brown, M. L. (1992). How chairpersons enhance faculty research: A grounded theory study. *Review of Higher Education, 16*(1), 41-62.

Creswell, J. W., et al. (1990). *The academic chairperson's handbook.* Lincoln, NE: University of Nebraska Press.

Daly, F., & Townsend, B. K. (1994). The chair's role in tenure acquisition. *Thought & Action: The NEA Higher Education Journal, 9* (2), 125-145.

Davidson, C. I., & Ambrose, S. A. (1994). *The new professor's handbook: A guide to teaching and research in engineering and science.* Bolton, MA: Anker.

Davis, B. G. (1993). *Tools for teaching.* San Francisco, CA: Jossey-Bass.

Diamond, R. M. (1994). *Serving on promotion and tenure committees: A faculty guide.* Bolton, MA: Anker.

Diamond, R. M. (1995). *Preparing for promotion and tenure review: A faculty guide.* Bolton, MA: Anker.

Diamond, R. M. (1998). *Designing & assessing courses & curricula: A practical guide.* San Francisco, CA: Jossey-Bass.

Diamond, R. M. (1999). *Aligning faculty rewards with institutional mission.* Bolton, MA: Anker.

Diamond, R. M., Adam, B. E., Froh, R. C., Gray, P. J., & Lambert, L. M. (Eds.). (1993). *Representing faculty work: The professional portfolio, 81.* San Francisco, CA: Jossey-Bass.

Downs-Lombardi, J. (1996). Ten teaching tips for newcomers. *College Teaching 44* (2), 62-63.

Eble, K. E. (1990). *The craft of teaching: A guide to mastering the professor's art* (2nd ed.). San Francisco, CA: Jossey-Bass.

Eble, K., & McKeachie, W. J. (1986). *Improving undergraduate education through faculty development.* San Francisco, CA: Jossey-Bass.

Edgerton, R. (1993). The tasks faculty perform. *Change, 24* (4), 4-6.

Education Commission of the States. (1996). What research says about improving undergraduate education: Twelve attributes of good practice. *AAHE Bulletin, 48* (8), 5-8.

Edwards, R. (1994). Toward a constructive review of disengaged faculty. *AAHE Bulletin, 47* (2), 6-7,11.

Fairweather, J. S. (1996). *Faculty work and the public trust.* Boston, MA: Allyn & Bacon.

Fink, L. D. (Ed.). (1984). *The first year of college teaching.* New Directions for Teaching and Learning, No. 17. San Francisco, CA: Jossey-Bass.

Fink, L. D. (1992). Orientation programs for new faculty. In M. D. Sorcinelli & A. E. Austin, (Eds.), *Developing new and junior faculty.* New Directions for Teaching and Learning, No. 50. San Francisco, CA: Jossey-Bass.

Finkel, S. K., Olswang, S., & She, N. (1994). Childbirth, tenure and promotion for faculty women. *The Review of Higher Education, 17* (3), 259-270.

Gaff, J. G., & Lambert, L. M. (1996). Socializing future faculty to the values of undergraduate education. *Change, 28* (4), 38-45.

Gibson, G. W. (1992). *Good start: A guidebook for new faculty in liberal arts colleges.* Bolton, MA: Anker.

Glassick, C. E., Huber, M. T., & Maeroff, G. I. (1997). *Scholarship assessed: Evaluation of the professoriate.* San Francisco, CA: Jossey-Bass.

Gmelch, W. H. (1993). *Coping with faculty stress.* Newbury Park, CA: Sage.

Gmelch, W. H., & Miskin, V. D. (1993). *Leadership skills for department chairs.* Bolton, MA: Anker.

Gmelch, W. H., & Miskin, V. D. (1995). *Chairing an academic department.* Thousand Oaks, CA: Sage.

Gmelch, W. H. (1996). It's about time. *Academe, 82* (5), 22-26.

Gmelch, W. H., Burns, J.B., Carroll, J.B., Harris, S., & Wentz, D. (1992). *Center for the Study of the Department Chair: 1990 Survey.* Pullman, WA: Washington State University.

Golde, C. M. (1999). After the offer, before the deal. *ACADEME, 85* (1), 44-49.

Grunert, J. (1997). *The course syllabus: A learning-centered approach.* Bolton, MA: Anker.

Gullette, M. M. (1992, March/April). Leading discussion in lecture courses: Some maxims and an exhortation. *Change,* 32-39.

Higgerson, M. L. (1996). *Communication skills for department chairs.* Bolton, MA: Anker.

Hirsh, D. (1996). An agenda for involving faculty in service. *AAHE Bulletin, 48* (9), 7-9.

Hitchcock, M. A., Bland, C. J., Hekelman, F. P., & Blumenthal, M. G. Academic success of faculty. *Academic Medicine, 70* (12), 1108-1116.

Hoag-Sowers, K., & Harrison, D. F. (1998). *Finding an academic job.* Thousand Oaks, CA: Sage.

Hutchings, P. (1993, November/December). Windows on practice: Cases about teaching and learning. *Change,* 14-21.

Hutchings, P. (1996). *Making teaching community property: A menu for peer collaboration and peer review.* Washington, DC: AAHE.

Hutchings, P. (1996). The pedagogical colloquium: Focusing on teaching in the hiring process. *AAHE Bulletin, 49* (3), 3-4.

Innovative Higher Education. (1996). Special issue on Peer Review of Teaching. *20* (4), 219-307.

Jarvis, D. K. (1991). *Junior faculty development: A handbook.* New York, NY: The Modern Language Association.

Kolodny, A. (1994, spring). Personal interview.

Leaming, D. R. (1998). *Academic leadership: A practical guide to chairing the department.* Bolton, MA: Anker.

Light, R. J. (1992). *The Harvard Assessment Seminars, Second Report: Explorations with students and faculty about teaching, learning, and student life.* Cambridge, MA: Harvard University, Graduate School of Education and Kennedy School of Government.

Lucas, A. F. (1989). Motivating faculty to improve the quality of teaching. In A. F. Lucas (Ed.), *The department chairperson's role in enhancing college teaching, 37,* 5-15. San Francisco, CA: Jossey-Bass.

Lucas, A. F. (1994). *Strengthening departmental leadership: A team-building guide for chairs in colleges and universities.* San Francisco, CA: Jossey-Bass.

Lynton, E. A. (1995). *Making the case for professional service.* Washington, DC: AAHE.

Marchese, T. J. (1987). *The search committee handbook: A guide to recruiting administrators.* Washington, DC: AAHE.

Massy, W. F., Wilger, A. K., & Colbeck, C. (1994). Overcoming "hollowed" collegiality. *Change, 26* (4), 10-20.

McKeachie, W. J. (1994). *Teaching tips: Strategies, research, and theory for college and university teachers* (9th ed.). Lexington, MA: D. C. Heath and Company.

Menges, R. J. & Associates. (1999). *Faculty in new jobs: A guide to settling in, becoming established, and building institutional support.* San Francisco, CA: Jossey-Bass.

Metter, E. (1996). Scholars in search of publishers. *AAHE Bulletin, 49* (3), 7-9.

Moody, J. (1997). *Demystifying the profession: Helping junior faculty succeed.* New Haven, CT: University of New Haven Press.

Murray, J. P. (1993). Hiring: Back to the basics. *The Department Chair, 3* (4), 16-17.

Neumann, A. (1993, April). The ties that bind: Notes on professorial colleagueship as academic context. Paper presented at the American Educational Research Association.

Nilson, L. B. (1998). *Teaching at its best: A research-based resource for college instructors.* Bolton, MA: Anker.

Olsen, D., & Sorcinelli, M. D. (1992). The pretenure years: A longitudinal perspective. In M. D. Sorcinelli & A. E. Austin (Eds.), *Developing new and junior faculty, 50,* 15-25. San Francisco, CA: Jossey-Bass.

Ory, J. C., & Ryan, K. E. (1993). *Tips for improving testing and grading.* Newbury Park, CA: Sage.

Palmer, P. J. (1993, November/December). Good talk about teaching: Improving teaching through conversation and community. *Change,* 8-13.

Pascarella, E., & Terenzini, P. (1991). *How college affects students.* San Francisco, CA: Jossey Bass.

Perlman, B., & McCann, L. I. (1996). *Recruiting good college faculty: Practical advice for a successful search.* Bolton, MA: Anker.

Pugh, K. L., Dinham, S. M. (1997). *The structure of stress in newly hired junior faculty.* Paper presented at the annual meeting of the American Educational Research Association. Chicago, Illinois.

Reynolds, A. (1992). Charting the changes in junior faculty: Relationships among socialization, acculturation, and gender. *Journal of Higher Education, 63* (6), 637-652.

Roberts, R. (1996). A report from the Stanford History Department. *AAHE Bulletin, 49* (3), 3-6.

Rodrigues, R. J. (1993, Summer). Translating your department culture for junior faculty. *The Department Chair, 4* (1), 9-10.

Rose, M. (1989). *Lives on the boundary.* New York, NY: Penguin Books.

Scott, R. R. (1981). Black faculty productivity and interpersonal academic contacts. *Journal of Negro Education, 50* (3), 224- 236.

Seagren, A. T., Creswell, J. W., & Wheeler, D. W. (1993). *The department chair: New roles, responsibilities and challenges.* Higher Education Report Number 1. Washington, DC: ASHE-ERIC.

Seldin, P. (1988). How colleges evaluate teaching: 1988 versus 1998. *AAHE Bulletin, 50* (7), 3-7.

Seldin, P. (1997). *The teaching portfolio: A practical guide to improved performance and promotion/tenure decisions* (2nd ed.). Bolton, MA: Anker.

Seldin, P. & Associates. (1999). *Changing practices in evaluating teaching: A practical guide to improved faculty performance and promotion/tenure decisions.* Bolton, MA: Anker.

Shulman, L. S. (1993). Teaching as community property: Putting an end to pedagogical solitude. *Change, 25* (6), 6-7.

Sorcinelli, M. D. (1989). Chairs and the development of new faculty. *The Department Advisor, 5* (2), 1-4.

Sorcinelli, M. D. (1992). New and junior faculty stress: Research and responses. In M. D. Sorcinelli & A. E. Austin (Eds.), *Developing new and junior faculty* (pp. 27-37). San Francisco, CA: Jossey Bass.

Sorcinelli, M. D. (1994). Effective approaches to new faculty development. *Journal of Counseling Development, 72,* 474-487.

Sorcinelli, M. D. (1999, Summer). New Pathways II: The tenure process. *The Department Chair, 10* (1), 3-4.

Svinicki, M., & O'Reilly, M. (1996). When faculty try quality: Three examples from the "Quality Teaching Project" at the University of Texas. *AAHE Bulletin, 49* (3), 10-13.

Thompson, C. J., & Dey, E. L. (1998). Pushed to the margins: Sources of stress for African American college and university faculty. *The Journal of Higher Education, 69* (3), 324-345.

Thyer, B. A. (1994). *Successful publishing in scholarly journals.* Thousand Oaks, CA: Sage.

Tierney, W. G., & Bensimon, E. M. (1996). *Promotion and tenure: Community and socialization in academe.* Albany, NY: SUNY Press.

Tierney, W. G., & Rhoads, R. A. (1994). *Faculty socialization as a cultural process: A mirror of institutional commitment.* ASHE-ERIC Higher Education Report No. 93-6. Washington, DC: The George Washington University School of Education and Human Development.

Tinto, V. (1987). *Leaving college: Rethinking the causes and cures of student attrition.* Chicago, IL: University of Chicago Press.

Tucker, A. (1992). *Chairing the academic department: Leadership among peers* (2nd ed.). New York, NY: ACE/Oryx.

Turner, C., Sotello, V., & Myers, Jr., S. L. (2000). *Faculty of color in academe: Bittersweet success.* Boston, MA: Allyn and Bacon.

Watson, G., et al. (1994). Pursuing a comprehensive faculty development program: Making fragmentation work. *Journal of Counseling and Development, 72* (5), 465-473.

Weimer, M. (1990). *Improving college teaching: Strategies for developing instructional effectiveness.* San Francisco, CA: Jossey-Bass.

Weimer, M. (Ed.). (1993). *Faculty as teachers: Taking stock of what we know.* State College, PA: National Center on Postsecondary Teaching, Learning, & Assessment.

Weimer, M. (1996). *Improving your classroom teaching.* Newbury Park, CA: Sage.

Wergin, J. F. (1993, July/August). Departmental awards. *Change, 24.*

Wergin, J. F. (1994). *The collaborative department: How five campuses are inching toward cultures of collective responsibility.* Washington, DC: AAHE.

Wergin, J. F. (1999, Spring). New Pathways II: The changing academic climate. *The Department Chair, 9* (4), 3-4.

Whicker, M. L., Kronefeld, J. J., & Strickland, R. A. (1993). *Getting tenure* (Vol. 8). Newbury Park, CA: Sage.

Whitt, E. J. (1991). Hit the ground running: Experiences of new faculty in a school of education. *Review of Higher Education, 14* (2), 177-197.

Wisconsin, University of (1998). *Peer review of teaching.* University of Wisconsin-Madison. Available: www.wisc.edu/MOO.

INDEX